SANDRA SHAMAS

A TRILOGY OF PERFORMANCES

THE MERCURY PRESS

The publisher gratefully acknowledges the financial assistance of the Canada Council for the Arts and the Ontario Arts Council.

The editor thanks Barbara Carey.

Cover design by Gordon Robertson
Cover photograph by Edward Gajdel
Edited by Beverley Daurio
Composition and page design by TASK

Printed and bound in Canada by Metropole Litho
Printed on acid-free paper
First Edition
1 2 3 4 5   01 00 99 98 97

Canadian Cataloguing in Publication Data

Shamas, Sandra, 1957–
Sandra Shamas : a trilogy of performances
My boyfriend's back and there's gonna be laundry — My boyfriend's back and there's gonna be laundry II: the cycle continues — Wedding bell hell
ISBN 1-55128-044-2
1. Canadian wit and humour (English).★ I. Title. II. Title: Trilogy of performances.
PS8587.H322S52 1997   C818'.5402   C97-932039-9
PR9199.3.S52S52 1997

Represented in Canada by the Literary Press Group
Distributed in Canada by General Distribution Services

THE MERCURY PRESS
2569 DUNDAS STREET WEST
TORONTO, ONTARIO
CANADA M6P 1X7

The words in this book are dedicated to Frank,
no matter what.

*I did not want to write this book. I did not want to let go of
these three shows. I wanted to keep them inside me forever so
I could hold them and have them. Because I knew if I let
them go, put them into a book, they would go into the hands
of others and have a life all their own. It's like watching your
children get on the school bus for the first time, and accepting
that they will have a life that you will not be a part of. I had
to accept that this was to happen, in order for me to move on.
I let them go with love.
Special thanks to Bev Daurio, who helped me let go of
my "children."*

Introduction

On my twenty-ninth birthday,

in 1986, I was in New York City and I saw Lily Tomlin perform at the Plymouth Theatre. I watched one woman command an audience of about seven hundred people for two-and-a-quarter hours. She was amazing. All she had on stage were two chairs and a riser of steps, and her remarkable talent. I watched this woman, and when I was finished watching, I thought to myself, *I could do that, in my own way.*

In 1987, I was about to turn thirty years old, and I was experiencing a lot of change. I affectionately refer to this time in my life as the "shit or get off the pot" period. I knew that whatever I had been doing before in terms of work, in terms of expression, I could do no more. I had to find something that would allow me to be me. And so, to that end, I applied to the Edmonton Fringe Festival, sent in my $300, and told them that the name of my show was *My Boyfriend's Back and There's Gonna Be Laundry.* They accepted my money and my application and told me that I had six performances. Unfortunately, I hadn't written the show yet.

So that August, while flying to Edmonton on Canadian Air, I wrote the show I was about to perform. And by writing, I mean I simply jotted down in point form the stories from my past that were important to me. I had never done a one-woman show. I had never stood on stage for more than six minutes alone. And I was quite terrified. When I got to Edmonton, my lower back seized, and I was hobbling to my tech at rehearsal when I noticed a tent in the fairgrounds with "*Ahhh*" on the side. The sound of relief! I hobbled into the tent, and there were

9

four massage therapists sitting around. And for five bucks, you could get a quick massage! So I lay on the table, told the woman what my problem was, told her why I was in Edmonton and what I was trying to do, and as she rubbed my lower back, she said, *Oftentimes, when we're frightened, we manifest our fear somewhere in our bodies. Classically speaking, pain in the lower back that inhibits movement is considered to be the fear of moving forward.* And that's what I was about to do. Move into a world I could never have imagined, and could only dare to hope for.

I sold out six shows in Edmonton with a performance that was fifty minutes long. I still actually find that quite remarkable, since I didn't know what I was doing. I just knew I had to do it.

Why three shows? Because no one will sit through one six-hour show. So I made three. And they came at their own pace. This work chronicles my life, its events, my relationships, my past and my present. And now this work in book form represents the future.

This book is thirty years of a life, nine years of a relationship, and the first seven years of my career. And it's only one-hundred-and-sixty pages!

So, welcome to my words. I hope they make you laugh.

Sandra Shamas

My Boyfriend's Back and There's
Gonna Be Laundry

I'd like to start the evening off by

offering you a performance art piece.

I'm holding in my hands a sturdy pair of men's cotton briefs. This is what men call "delicates." Quickly now, a fashion tour. Not for the faint of heart, I might add.

Right off the top, huge, nuclear-resistant elastic. Now I'm going to stretch this elastic as far as it can go... See how big your belly can get? This would have been in evidence on Thanksgiving. Also, a note before we move on: this is usually the last item left standing before a man goes and buys new underwear.

Next, the leg area. Now, they don't put elastic into the leg area of men's underwear. No, they put this very user-friendly cotton ribbing action. But, as we all well know, after repeated washings, this area tends to stretch out quite a bit, making way for the often heard, summer-time phrase, "Oh man, my bag is everywhere."

Next, the opening. The "pocket." There she is— knock knock knock— and nobody's home. I'm thirty-seven years old. I've lived on the planet earth most of those years and I've learned, just recently, that men don't even use it. And it's always on the right-hand side. Well, what if you're left-handed? What? Do you ask the guy next to you to go in for you? You know, if purses were ever outlawed, women could wear these and just put everything we need right in there.

Last, and certainly not least, this area here below the pocket. This area *right* here is colloquially known as "the basket."

Yes.

"Hooters."

"Basket."

Now, many of you won't even recognize these; so nice and flat and, *white*, like this. Maybe I can help you recognize them, if I wad them up into a tight angry little ball. Maybe you'll recognize them better in their natural habitat: the floor.

On the cover of every

Cosmopolitan magazine published is a photograph of a woman. You are familiar with this magazine? Helen Gurley Brown is the editor-in-chief of *Cosmopolitan* magazine, who, I personally think, looks a lot like Tutankhamen. Notice how they're never seen together. Helen says that the woman who is on the front cover of *Cosmopolitan* magazine is a fair representation of the woman of today. So, there's our representative on the front cover of *Cosmo*— big hair, big tits, back arched, with a pre-orgasmic look on her face— this, as you know, is a natural pose for women. Perhaps many of you have found yourself in *exactly* this same pose? You know, you're at the bank, for instance, standing in the line-up, waiting and waiting, and suddenly, without a moment's notice, your hair gets bigger, your tits jut out, and your butt hits the guy behind you...

Oh, but it gets better. We're so well-represented on television, I'm sure many of you identify heavily with women on TV. I know I do. The women who have straight hair. Straight, perfect hair. Little blunt cuts. And the hair actually never moves. But the head within the hair moves. And she's holding some dishwashing detergent, and she's way too excited. Do you know why? Because the product *actually washes more dishes*. What the fuck is wrong with you? I want to wash way *less* dishes. Why even invite that shit into your home?

Okay, have you seen this ad? The first thing that happens on the screen is that there's a big honking pad, so huge that it's actually real-estate at this point, and you see the big honking pad and then you see a woman's hand with an eye-dropper in it. And then there's that blue water, which we all possess, and she's writing "Always" with the eye-dropper on the pad. I thought it was a sanitary pad, not a note-pad. Next thing you know you'll find these things stuck to the refrigerator with "I've gone to the store" written on four of them.

Then there's those tall, elegant women with their hair wrapped in a chignon. Do you know this hair-do? It looks like a huge croissant gone bad on the back of her head. And it's perfect and she's wearing something off-white and flowing, and she's holding a box of Playtex tampons. "Playtex tampons with the plastic applicator, they're so much more comfortable than the cardboard ones." Hey! I don't keep the applicator in there. You can make it out of zinc if you like.

And she's wearing... *white*. Come on, what's the rule, girls? The rule is simply this:

Never wear white on day two.

Unless you'd like to chance that the back of your skirt will look like the flag of Japan.

Ever hear of the pad with wings? The Pegasus of pads?

Follow the evolution. The first sanitary napkin was so large that if you were wearing one, and you sat down, you were three inches taller than everybody else. Then, they made them really thin. And they wanted us to thank them. For what? For finally inventing a pad that didn't make me look like I was smuggling a canoe in my pants?

Then, they put wings on the fucking things. So when they introduced this product, pads with wings, they had to use scientific credibility to sell it to us, you know, 'cause we're not dumb, eh? We won't just slap *anything* down there. I remember watching the ad on TV, and them dragging out an animated grid from NASA. I guess they'd been doing some wind tunnel experiments with the pad. And then, on this animated grid, they had a drawing of the old wingèd pad. And before your very eyes, it starts to flap and buck like a little pony. What if that actually started happening in your pants? "Whoa, whoa, Flicka!... Whoa, girl!"

Could be a new method of commuting.

"How'd you get here?"

"Took the five o'clock pad."

Whenever they want to sell us sanitary products, they find the most serene, robust, brunette with doe eyes. And she's got that deer-caught-in-the-headlights look... And she's walking really serenely through a field of wheat, wearing an off-white hand-knit sweater, smelling a daisy...

I NEVER FEEL LIKE THAT WHEN I'M HAVING MY PERIOD!

Why don't they pull up a shot of some bloated dolphins on a beach somewhere?

It's a well-known fact amongst women that when a group of women cluster together for a length of time, eventually all of them will have their periods— (CLAP!)— at exactly the same time. Do you know this? Do you know the name of it? I found out recently, it's called The Genevieve Effect. So, for those of you who have never experienced this first hand, go to a restaurant some time where all the waitresses who work there have done so since 1971, and you stumble in on THAT Wednesday. And, for sure, all the waitresses will come at you screaming, "WHY ARE YOU HERE AND WHAT THE HELL DO YOU WANT?"

I think that this particular thing amongst women is exactly why they don't allow us into combat. Well, imagine a battalion of armed, pre-menstrual, women.

I mean, if there wasn't a fight, we'd pick one.

And then we'd win.

I was born and raised in

a small northern Ontario mining community called Sudbury.
Sudbury is four-hundred-and-fifty miles north of Toronto.
Sudbury is a mining community, and the only reason the city
exists is because of the mine. One day they discovered a reason
to mine— they discovered nickel— and then they made this
big hole in the ground. And you know how a hole can attract
men...

So, when I was growing up in Sudbury, it was very
masculine. It was the kind of place where all the men were...
MEN!

And all the women were... MEN!

Short stocky women with mannish haircuts and club jackets
in Sudbury are not lesbians. They're hockey moms. You will
make a lot of mistakes, as a lesbian, cruising rinks in Sudbury.

In Sudbury, you know a man is going to be a sensitive lover
if he takes his socks off.

"Hey, aren't you going to take your socks off?"

"No. I might have to go for a whiz."

So in Sudbury, when a man asked you out on a date— with
words— there were only a couple of places to go, and they
were both bars. You could go to the bar, and drink, or you
could go to the Legion Hall, and drink. The Legion Hall, I
don't know if you know this, originally was a place for veterans
to go and commune after the war, and they'd have dances and
social events. But, you know, I'd love to have gone there in its
hey-day, 'cause by the time I got to the Legion I just thought
it was a place where toothless men ate pickled eggs.

So, we go to the bar. I want you to know, I made an effort. I was wearing a pair of green, pinwale cords with a huge flare that dragged on the ground, and they were all chewed out at the back. White, angora sweater on top. We go to the bar. All the bars are pretty much the same. They have round, copper-topped pedestal tables, and we're sitting at one. The guy that I'm with is slouched, legs akimbo, and he's doing that man thing where one leg is constantly jittering.

Suddenly he's still. His arm shoots into the air over his head, and he snaps his fingers and yells, "HEY! LUCY!" to get the waitress's attention. He draws a full circle in the air over the table with his finger, sticks one thumb up to Lucy, and she nods, confirming the transaction.

This is affectionately known as "letting the man order."

Over comes Lucy. She's about four-foot-nothing and can bench-press seven hundred pounds, and she has got on her hand a tray that is exactly the same size as the table, and it's loaded with glasses filled with amber liquid called draft beer that has an alcohol content that would kill a bull moose. I think the table held thirty glasses. And we're going to drink all of it, because this is our first date.

Now in Sudbury, for a woman to be a MAN, you have to drink, toe for toe, drink for drink, shot for shot, beer for beer, with the guy. But you must never, under any circumstances, appear drunk. Because if a man in Sudbury sees that you are drunk, he will jump on you and hump your leg. This is as unattractive as it sounds. So as a result, the women in Sudbury can drink like... MARINES!, and still maintain a womanly demure. But women know, women know when one another are drunk. Women know. And here's one of the very first tell-tale signs... You're drunk. You're trying to act really smooth. You go to take a sip and you rake your teeth with the rim of the glass. It's like drunken wind chimes. The second one is... when you're so drunk you forget to stop talking when you're about to take a drink. You're still blathering away— that beautiful drunken blather— at the same time you're pouring beer down your throat. It's an input-output challenge. You'll either drown or find all the words swirling around the bottom of the glass.

So there we are. We're drinkin', we're drinkin', we're drinkin', and, you know, he's startin' to look a lot better.

Sudbury, because it's a mining community, has a smelter. They take the rock out of the ground. They send it to the smelter, and through the smelting process they extract nickel, copper, silver, zinc... some gold, and precious metals. They take that right out of the rock through the smelting process, and they send all that good stuff down to the United States of America, and we Sudburians, and more collectively, Canadians, are left with huge amounts of useless molten rock called *slag*. Depending on the day's production, they can fill five to twenty two-hundred-ton cauldrons full of slag and send them along a railway track out to a predestined hill. Then, at a certain time every night, they pour the slag. And that's all that happens. These huge cauldrons dump their contents down these blackened hills and the slag pours down these *huge* hills, and it looks for all the world like thin streams of lava. It does. The red heat rises, interferes with the atmosphere, and everything around for a two-mile radius takes on an orangey, smoky, hue.

We Sudburians take advantage of this man-made phenomenon... to neck.

We're back at the bar and we've been drinking really heavily. I mean table after table of draft has come and gone. We're shit-faced for sure. I mean, we're too drunk to walk... so we drive.

And he has an excellent car... a Duster. And there's flames painted down the side. I know you want him. So we get into the Duster and we go and we park at the parking lot that overlooks the dump site. It's all very organized. They put in that parking lot at the side of the dump because you cannot park at the bottom of the slag... It's a great view. But it's the last one you'll see.

Now, say you go to Sudbury, say— just say— you might go, I don't know. Say you go, and you're in the mood to neck. God, who wouldn't be? Don't be necking at the slag before it pours. No. Cool your lips. Wait for that slag to pour.

Now that's *ambience*.

I'm sitting on the passenger side of the Duster, and the Duster has a sofa seat, and three on the tree. And it's pitch black, and my eyes are jiggling in my head from the booze. That's a good look for a woman. And I'm sitting there thinking, *I wonder how he'll start? I wonder how he's gonna start?* He's gotta start somehow. How's he gonna get his lips from way over there to way over here? Maybe he'll do that thing, like guys do at the movies: big yawn and stretch, arm moving laterally until the hand finds its way around your shoulder. Or maybe he'll do that thing guys do in the movies, where they grab your whole face by the chin and kiss the woman hard on the mouth... Owww. That would hurt.

So I'm sitting there contemplating these possibilities, and I look up and notice that they've started to pour the slag. And before you can say, "Oh, look, they've started to pour the slag," he jumps me.

Now we're necking and necking, necking, neck, neck... We're necking over here, and we're necking over there. Here a neck, there a neck, everywhere a neck, neck...

We're necking.

If you've ever necked in the front seat of a vehicle for any length of time, inevitably your face gets squooshed into the door and you get those tell-tale knob marks on your face. God, that really hurts.

So, there we are. We're necking up a storm and that slag's pouring. It just doesn't get more beautiful. And, suddenly, he starts to serpentine his hand up the back of my sweater. Na na na— *Na*. Na na na— *Na*. I don't know why, but all I can hear is the theme music from *My Three Sons*. Now, we're still necking like cats in heat, but my brain is going *beboo beboo beboo*. Skin to skin, skin to skin. Looks like he's going after... (CLAMP!)... the BRA-STRAP!

Okay. He's locked on. And he's started doing that excellent little manoeuvre that guys do when they try to undo your bra-strap with only one hand, showing that they're ever so suave. But this guy's not a DeVry graduate. He's working at it, and we're still necking, and he's got both his hands in there now, and he's really reefing on it, and his mouth slides half off mine, and he's kissing and swearing and sweating...

HEY! I'M BLEEDING FROM THE SPINE!

And as he's yanking on the strap, the "girls" are swinging back and forth... TITS ARE NOT MEANT TO TRAVEL! Clearly an emergency situation. So, I think I'm doing the womanly, demure thing, and I just... n'dge him. Not PUSH. And then I undo my own bra-strap and I clamp my ARMS DOWN for EVERYTHING I'M WORTH. (Suddenly, I'm Miss Jean Brodie: "Aye, you can have the strap, but you're no' gettin' to the girrrls.")

The Girls: Häagen and Dazs. The bigger one got the bigger name. I named my breasts because men name their dicks. Here are the best two names for a man's dick I've ever heard in my life. The first one was: "The Humiliator." And the second one was: "Big Steve and the Twins."

Now, I have a huge fear. I have a huge fear. I have a huge fear that my bra is going to pop up like a venetian blind— FLAP! FWWWWP! You see, whenever you look at a women's magazine and you see the torso of a nude woman, all these models have those perfect little ski-jump tits. And the nipple is way the fuck up around her neck somewhere!

Not me. I was blessed with a set of east-westerlies. (They would not make good tracking dogs.) Once released from their cottony confines, they kinda slide down my chest in opposite directions, complaining bitterly all the way, "Oh-h-h-h, fuck, it was hot in there today, eh?" So, as you can well imagine, I don't unleash them at will.

So now I'm back on the passenger side, I've got my arms clamped down, and I'm all freaked out and sweatin' that sweat, that weird sweat that smells like burning hair, you know what I mean, like you took two dead mallards and tucked them under your armpits kinda sweat. And I'm so preoccupied with myself, I don't even notice he's pushed himself all the way back over to the driver's side. He's looking out the window. And his jaw's clenched. He's mad. He's mad, and you know, it actually looks like his feelings have been hurt. It's hard to imagine a single-celled being with hurt feelings.

He starts up the Duster and we start driving away. This is a very bumpy road, so I jam my one arm up my back and do up my own bra-strap with one hand. And we drive in silence. That kind of silence men make. Maybe you know it. It's not even silence, it's more like the absence of sound. And you know women— right there to fill a void... "Well, whatIwasthinkin-gofdoingwasgoingdown... andyouknowwhatIwasgoingtotell-her..."

We pull up in front of my parents' place.

Silence.

"Um... are you mad?..."

He looks over blankly.

"Um, are you mad 'cause I undid my own bra-strap?"

Silence.

"Maybe."

"Because I thought that was what you were trying to do, and I was just tryin' to help?"

"I didn't want your help. I wanted to do it myself."

I see. I'm just Bra-Strap 101 to this guy. So I left the car, thinking, *You wanted to do it yourself?* And I was so fucking mad. I didn't have that saucy little retort, right then and there. Have you ever been in a situation where you wish you had a perfect comeback, a perfect little thing to say? Fourteen years later at three o'clock in the morning I thought of the most perfect thing to say. I should have just turned to him right then and said,

"You know, you should have stayed home and done it yourself."

Hey, I thought it was damn saucy at the time.

The very first job I ever had

was at the Bamboo Gardens, The Home of Fine Canadian and Chinese Cuisine. Now, allow me to define Chinese food in northern Ontario. When you ordered chicken fried rice, it was always served with lovely hot buttered toast.

You don't just go for the rice.

I wore a very fetching uniform. It was black polyester. And that good poly. You know, not that bad poly. It had a vee-neck, a notched collar and an empire waist. There was gold piping on the collar to maintain an oriental motif, and the short sleeve had a hole cut out of it and a button, peek-a-boo style, if you will, 'cause everybody knows that's the best part of a woman. And I wore that fetching outfit with taupe pantyhose and white patent leather nurse shoes. If they got hit with sweet and sour sauce, they'd wipe up in a jiffy. I was wearing this festive ensemble in 1977 when the King died. Do you know what you were wearing when Elvis died?

Sudbury has a huge French–Canadian population. Over 60% of the people who live there are French-speaking. One night after shift, my best friend Sherry and I decided to go to see a movie. So I called up the Odeon Theatre to find out what was playing and I said,

"Hi, yeah, can you tell me what's on tonight?"

And the woman who answered the phone said, "Oui... tonight... Stylvester Stallony en *FISS*, puis *Honey Owl*."

"Hello? Ah, can you please repeat that? Because I didn't even get a chance to write it down. I'm sorry."

"Stylvester..."

"Okay."

"Stallony..."

"Uh huh."

"En *FISS*."

"Is there a 'T' at the end of that?"

"Oui. Puis *Honey Owl*."

"Okay. That one. I didn't get it all..."

"J'ai dit! *Honey... Owl*."

"Honey. Honey. Owl...? Okay, thanks a lot."

I hang up.

Sherry says, "What's on?"

I look at what I've written.

"Stylvester Stallony in *FIST*... and *Honey Owl*."

"*Honey Owl*?"

"I swear to God, Sherry. That's what she said. I wrote it down. Look, Sherry. *Honey Owl*."

Sherry said, "That's insane. *Annie Hall* is playing there."

"Annie Hall? Annie Hall!?" So I said, "Sherry, I must see this woman with my very own eyes."

We jumped in her dad's truck,

drove down to the city centre and there, at the entrance to the Odeon Theatre, behind a plexiglas containment, with a wicket just for your hand, was the most remarkable woman I have ever seen in my life.

She was perched... PERCHED, on her Odeon stool. More like nailed to it, more like they built the place around her. She had a very form-fitting Odeon outfit, cat's-eye glasses with rhinestones at the edge, and the biggest, swear to God, free-standing, platinum blonde, beehive hair-do in the Nickel Belt Area, I am sure. Through pursed lips, she says to me,

"Oui. Can I 'elp you?"

"Yeah. Yes. Two for *Honey Owl*, please."

This woman would come into the Bamboo Gardens and I would run to serve her. She wasn't hard to find, her hair was like a monolith. I found out her name. Her name was Louise Tranche-Montagne.

"You know, that's a fascinating last name. Is there a meaning to that at all?"

"Oui. De firs' part, de Tranche, dat's like a slice, eh? De las' part, Montagne, slice. Slice-of-de-mountain."

"That's beautiful."

I got to know this woman. Wouldn't you? Louise was one of a breed of woman who was incredibly independent. Fiercely independent. Remarkably opinionated. At the point when I knew her, she had never married, and, you know, it didn't look like marriage was going to happen. But it didn't matter. Louise was just that kind of person. And nobody ever dicked with Louise ever, *ever*. Nobody ever fucked around with her. Her favourite expression was,

"EH! Don't you press my nerve."

And conversely, you know, she would sing at the drop of a hat. She loved to sing. She fancied herself a chanteuse. Her favourite song was, "Eh! Did you 'appen to see de most beautiful girl in de worl'? An' if you did, was it Louise Tranche-Montagne?"

So, one night I went over to Louise's place

and I was belly-aching that I didn't have a boyfriend, or something... or anything.

So, Louise says to me, "Don't mind me saying, eh? But you're never gonna get a man lookin' like dat. I can give you some advice, eh? But I don't give dis advice to just anybody, eh?

"Firs', go to de beauty parlour, eh? Get your hairs done like me. Comme ça. Be sure to get de bang on de front and de kiss-curl on de side. Dat way you can buy dat pink zig-zag tape and put dem on at night. Dey last forever.

"Next. Go to de K-Mart, and buy a nice pant-suit. You know de one I mean, eh? Le tunic, sleeveless. Dey have de gold button all de way down the front, comme ça. Dey're fake, eh?

Don't worry. Dere's a zipper up de back. And de pant, dey have de seam sewn down de front, comme ça. And buy bleu, eh? Dat way you can buy de matching eye-shadow, eh?

"Okay, d'abord. Go home, eh? Take your time. Nice. Nice. Take a nice bath, but don't mess your hairs, eh? Do like me, take de toilet paper, go around and around your hairs. Dat way, dey stay dry. Take a nice bath. Take your time. Nice. Nice.

"Get dressed. Nice. Put on d'eye-shadow, de blusher, de lipstick and... kabang!... you're ready to go to de Legion.

"Don't go to de Legion alone, eh? Tsk, tsk, tsk. A lady does not go to de Legion alone. I always go with my friend Solange.

"Go nice to de Legion. Nice. Go inside, nice, to de bar, get one beer, and get a glass, don't drink out of de bottle like a pig. Sit nice at de table. Pour de beer 'alf-way in de glass, comme ça. Make sure to 'ave a few cigarette already roll. Sit nice. Nice. Cross your legs. Wait nice for de man to come and ask you to dance and den... kabang!... he can buy your beers all night long."

What was even more startling about this advice was her success with it. Louise had a different date every Saturday night. And I was happy for her, but given where she was getting these guys, I mean, it was no surprise they were coming in on chains.

"Hey, Louise, he sits really nice. Hi, fella!"

"Oui. I got 'im at de Legion. C'mon!"

The only thing I've ever looked for

in my whole life was love. I've looked for one person to love, and to have that one person love me back. Crazy, isn't it? When I was a little kid I asked my Mom:

"Mom. Mom. Mom. Mom. Mom. Momma. Momma. Momma."

I'm yanking on her apron.

"Mom." Yank. "Mom. Momma. Momma." Yank. "Mom, how will I know I'm in love?"

"You'll know."

No, what part of the question didn't you understand?

"*How. How...* will I know I'm in love?"

"YOU'LL KNOW!"

And we'd had one of those lovely mother–daughter conversations.

From Sudbury I moved to Toronto.

Actually, I went first to Europe; I was looking for myself. I was not there. And then I moved to Toronto. Toronto had men. Men, men, men! It was like eye candy. And they were all beautiful, oh, my God.

Actually, I should preface this by telling you what the criteria for a man in Sudbury was. Very simple. Very simple criteria. Shirt on the top. Pants on the bottom. Accept no substitution.

One of the very first jobs I ever had in Toronto was as a bartender in a place called the Nag's Head Tavern. And I shared

31

the bartending duties with a woman by the name of Lorna. And every day, Lorna and I would watch the men come in. Oh, beautiful men, oh, my God. Men with parts in their hair. Sweater, matching socks. And, you know, women *do* look at men. We do look at men. Unlike men, we don't use our tongues. We use our eyes, incredibly enough. And we're very economical. Once up, once down...

I think that's what makes us good shoppers.

"Oh, my God! Did you see the basket on that guy?"

One day, Lorna and I are standing at the bar
watchin' the pay show (we called it the "pay show"). Just these beautiful men coming in, one by one.

Me, I'm oohing and ahing and getting an eyeful. Every now and then I'd give a nod to Lorna:

"Lorna! Incoming! Two o'clock, two o'clock!"

And Lorna says, "Sandy, dear. Can I see you down at the end of the bar, darlin'?"

Lorna always wore a gold smock with these big square pockets, and her glasses hung around her neck on a chain of fake pearls. She takes out a pack of smokes. She's got a butt there she's been saving since breakfast.

"Sandy, dear." She lights her butt. "Oh, Christ, I got fucking smoke in my eye. Them men you been oglin', dear. They're gay."

"No. No, they're not. No, please, no, they're not. Ah, c'mon!"

And I went into my "Oh, what a waste" phase.

"Oh, what a waste!"

And then I went into my, "Come home with me. You're sick. I'll fix you," phase. Try to imagine some poor gay guy sitting in my kitchen in a high chair, me force-feeding him chicken soup:

"Are you straight yet?"

I refer to this as my "learning to lose" period. 'Cause there I was. I was a single woman, in a *world class* city, and I didn't know how to meet people. And I didn't know how to meet men, and, I mean, that is for sure. I'm actually very shy. I mean, I'm not good at meeting people. I'm just not very good at it. Look what I do for a living, just to get out of the house!

It is the long, hot summer of '83,

and all the women I know are single. Now that's ugly. Really. Everybody's sitting around the table, smoking, drinking, and howling. It's very bad. And we're trying to think of where, where do you go to meet men? Well, what did they do fifty years ago? Fifty years ago they had barn raising and square dancing. They don't have square dancing any more, do they? No. People dancing around big barns, fresh-scrubbed, apple-cheeked boys leaning against the back wall going, "My, my. Doesn't Linda-Sue look mighty fetchin' tonight?" That's not fucking happening anywhere.

So where do you go? Where do you go? Do you go to a singles bar?

Gotta be the loneliest place in the world. Sit at the bar, go to the bar, sit at the bar. Order something off the "fun" placemat menu.

"Yeah, I'll have... ah... a sidecar. Does it come in a glass? Good. Okay, I'll have that."

Then what do you do? How do you introduce yourself to somebody? Do you wait for some guy to burn you with his cigarette?

"OWWW!"

"Oh, hi." Then what? Do you show him your tits?

I didn't know what to do. I even consulted *Cosmopolitan* magazine.

Now, *Cosmo* never tells you how to get someone new, but they've got lots of suggestions on what to do when you've got him. They had an article at the time entitled "The Eroticism of Bathing":

"Don't be afraid to throw herbs, ginger, even lettuce, in the tub."

"Well, get it up, Roy. There's two heads of romaine in there."

What a shameful waste of crudités. And then, what man in his right mind is going to step into a tub with *shit* floating in it? Oh, and ginger! There's a good suggestion. I'll just burn his dick off.

"Are you hot yet?"

"No? Here's some more ginger!"

So, *Cosmo* has lots of ideas about what to do, you know. They say, "When you go on a date, don't be afraid to wear red, strappy sandals and a gardenia in your hair." Could you look like a bigger asshole? I don't think so.

And you know, as an aside, *Cosmopolitan* has a little column that occasionally appears in the magazine, and it's a little column entitled "Why Don't You... ?" I don't know if you've ever seen this, but it is literally a list of activities for women. It's because we don't do enough. Yes. That's it. After all, I know you are just like me, and I stand around all day in my robe, staring off into the ionosphere and eating bon-bons.

So anyway, here are some of the suggestions they make to women:

Why Don't You... wake up at five in the morning, and clean your kitchen?

Why Don't You... have a gift-wrapping party?

Why Don't You... hug him? Even if he's cranky.

You know, chances are, if he's cranky, I made him that way. Now, there's an activity, eh?

So there I was. I was single and desperate

in a world class city. So I responded to an ad in the companions-wanted section of the alternative arts newspaper in Toronto called *NOW Magazine*.

I should let you know that at the time that I responded to the ad, they were still using whole words. Yeah. Now you read the personals, and it's like "SWM BM MN." Ah, c'mon! Buy a fucking vowel here!

So I've got *NOW Magazine* cracked open on the kitchen

table, and I'm whippin' down the column. And there it is. Screech to a halt. It's a little ad, but it's funny, and it makes me laugh. Humour is the first prerequisite: humour. For me, humour is the very first prerequisite. Even before having a dick. Because you might have a dick but you don't know what to do with it. In the event that you have a sense of humour, we could both laugh.

It's a funny ad. So I send off a funny card, because... I can. And I get a letter back from him and it's pretty amusing and his phone number's there, so I dial the number and he's not home. His answering machine is on and the message is actually pretty funny so, you know, I leave a few clever quips on there myself, because... I can. And, finally, this guy and I meet on the phone and we decide to get together for a drink.

I'm standing in front of the mirror. I'm wearing just a crisp white ensemble. And I'm putting on "d'eye-shadow, de blusher, de lipstick..." (Louise is never far.) And I'm out the door.

Now, it suddenly dawns on me, as I'm walking towards the café, that I've never seen this guy. I don't know what he looks like. And why has this crucial piece of information eluded me up until now? So as I'm walking down the street, I start to reason that any one of these critically *ugly* men could be him. I get to the café and I don't know what he looks like. So I start making meaningful eye contact with every lone guy in the place. Finally, as I'm standing there making an ass of myself, coming on to all the men in the restaurant, this guy stands up at the back of the room, turns around, and yells,

"HEY!"

Have you ever seen a thing in your life that made you want

to scream, but you couldn't? So I'm standing there twitching while my brain keeps repeating, "*RUN AWAY! RUN AWAY! RUN AWAY!*"

We are standing there *locked in horror* looking at one another. It's like we are both witnessing a genetic car accident at the same time. I wish there could have been thought bubbles over our heads so you could read what we were thinking.

'Cause I'm sure he's looking at me, thinking, *A little hairier, we get a leash, we take her for a walk.*

I'm looking at him, going, *Is it actually possible for the human cranium to be that small?*

I'm ready to run, when this voice comes out of the back of my head. I call her the piano teacher, but she's really the voice of reason.

And she says, in that patient, patronizing way, "Now, Sandra, I'm sure he's a lovely boy."

FUCK OFF!

I aim towards him. I get to the table. We sit across from each other. We have not ripped our eyes from each other.

Luckily, I smoked heavily at the time. I just lit the whole pack.

The waitress comes by.

I order: "I'll have a case of beer. Just put it at my feet."

Twenty-five of the most evil little minutes of my life went by.

And finally, I went, "Well, now, would you look at the time? Yes, I've got to dash. Really, I have to go home. I have to... um... um... smoke a ham."

I'm outta there.

Now, I'm on my way home, and I'm having my personal chat with the Lord. I press my palms together in front of me. (Speaking into my fingers: "Check! Check. Is this thing on?"):

"Dear God... first of all, thank you very much for all the health my family enjoys."

You have to start that way. Don't be begging and negative the whole time.

"And then, God, when it comes my time for a guy, pass me by. Go to the next person on the list. 'Cause I've fuckin' had it with men."

You know, at that point in my life I was still on the pill, for no reason. So, I decided to be single. Yes, I decided to be single.

Like I had a fucking choice.

Now, when you go to the magazine rack

and you see the entire world of magazines that are available to women, all these magazines are pretty much the same. They have a woman on the front cover and the headers to the articles inside them are on either side of her head. And these headers are there just to entice you into buying the magazine. So, you know, there's a wide variety of topics on each cover. You find "Fashion Tips for '94," "Thin Thighs in 30 Days," "Lose 30 Pounds in Two Weeks," or little psychological pieces like "Five Things Men Fear." (They're all premature ejaculation.)

Inevitably, on the front cover of one of these magazines, there'll be an article entitled something like, "The Joy of Being Single." Biggest oxymoron in the world. A contradiction in terms. Like "jumbo shrimp," "military intelligence" or "*Toronto Life.*"

Now, these articles are there to help you be better at being single. 'Cause you're just not doing a good enough job. And they make suggestions to single women like, "take brisk walks," and "don't be afraid to dine alone."

Have you ever done this? Have you ever dined alone?

Okay. You go. You're upright. You're bathed. You're dressed. You're standing in front of the "Please wait to be seated" sign. The hostess comes over with a fan of menus, and she gives you that "Oh, you-poor-piece-of-shit, you-couldn't-find-anybody-to-eat-with-you" look, takes you to a table for two by the toilet, hands you one menu, and then abandons you.

Because whatever you've got might be catching.

The waiter comes over. Big attitude.

"Can I get you a drink while you're *waiting?*"

For who? Godot?

And then he takes the other placemat away. The word "pathetic" lights up over your head.

Fuck that.

I eat over the sink. I dine alone with the sink. The nice, stainless steel placemat for one. I take the pot off the stove. I go to the sink. And I dine alone!

But when I decided to be single, I envisioned my singledom to be a lot more romantic. In my singleness, I was a little taller, and willowy. Okay, maybe decalcified is a better word. And I wore a lot of white, gauzy cotton clothes that wafted around me. And my hair was shorter, but tawny-coloured. And I don't even know what colour that is. But whenever I read a Harlequin romance, the heroine always has "green, flashing eyes, and tawny hair." I WANT IT!

And I'm wearing round, tortoise-shell framed glasses. And I can be found sitting alone in cafés, sipping an espresso with a twist of lemon, reading Jean-Paul Sartre, nauseating myself to death.

So, what happens? What happens?

You know, I turned my head away for a second, and into my life walks this guy.

The one.

He was, *the one*.

How did I know he was *the one*? Because when I looked at this guy, I heard an operatic version of *Star Trek* music in my head. He was tall and lean and blond, blue-eyed, funny, bright, articulate... and younger.

You get them young, you can train them.

And his name was Frank. I fell in love with Frank. Now, I don't know about you, but when I fall in love, I give my brain... AWAY.

Nobody— but especially other single women— wants to be around a woman who has just fallen in love. No. Well, you know why. It's because her voice goes up three octaves, it takes on a sickening sing-songy quality, and the sum total of her conversation is, "And then you know what else he said? And he's so funny, and he's so smart. And, also, he's not like any

man I've ever met before in my whole life. And he's so smart
and he's so funny. You know what he said?"

"AH, SHUT THE FUCK UP!"

So there I was. I was in love love love love love.

So, one day, the phone rings.

"Hello."

(It's Frank.)

"Hiyee. How are you? What? Oh, I'd love to get together.
It's so funny 'cause I was just thinking about you and then the
phone rings. Weird, eh?... What? No, let's get together. I'd love
that. Let's have coffee. Yeah... I know where it is... Yeah. I can
be there in fifteen minutes... No problem. Okay. Bye... What?
Oh, I'd love to talk to you, too... Okay... I'll see you there in
fifteen... Okay. Bye-bye..."

(Pause.)

"Uh? No, you hang up first..."

"Okay, we'll count together..."

"One... two..."

I go to the café. Frank is already there.

He is already sitting at a table for two. He has already ordered
coffee. He's very handsome. And so I go and sit across from him.

"Hello!"

And he says seriously, "Hi... um... thanks, ah... thanks very
much for coming."

41

"No trouble."

"Look, um... there's no easy way for me to say this..."

"Oh, then don't say it."

"Yeah, um... you know, ah... you know, I've, ah... I've been doing some thinking... and, ah... something I want you to know, it's not you, you know. But I really feel like things are going way too fast for me right now and I'm not ready, at all, to make any kind... of... emotional... com... mit... ment."

Well, sing along if you know the words.

And, you know, when somebody

levels shit like that at you, you think, *You can't be talking to me.* And you look around, and there's just nobody else there.

Right away all the blood in my body went *fffff*, right into my head, and I could hear my heart in my ears. And nausea.

And I'm looking right at him as hard as I can, I'm looking dead at him, and all I see is his mouth moving and no sound coming out.

"Oh, fuck. I'm getting dumped and I'm deaf, too."

That voice of the piano teacher comes out of the back of my head and says, "You don't let this bastard see you cry!"

Tears come. "I can't help it. I can't help it."

"STAND UP!"

"Okay. I'm up..."

"GO TO THE DOOR!"

"I don't know where the door is!"

"IT'S OVER THERE!"

"Oh, please. Please. What if he changes his mind?"

"HE HASN'T GOT A FUCKIN' MIND TO CHANGE! GET OUTTA HERE!"

"Oh, man... I am never going to get laid ever, ever, ever again..."

So, where do you go?

Where do you go when somebody says, "I'm not here for you any more? Sorry!"

Where do you go?

Well, I don't know about you, but I like to turn my head— down the path of self-destruction.

"Hi, is this the liquor store? Do you take VISA? Great! Do you deliver? Can I get a case of Jack Daniel's, please? Thank you."

I go to the store.

"Hi! Can I get a carton of Marlboros? I'll take a carton of Camels... Okay, give me a carton of Lucky Strike shit-ends... for the rasp... and I'll take a flat of... Snickers bars."

I'm diggin' in.

I'm diggin' in for Stinky Pyjama Time. Stinky Pyjama Time. Maybe you know it. It does not have to be pyjamas. It can be bad track pants with the pills all over them. Regardless, the outfit is a legged garment with the crotch way down around your knees. And you wear that with a completely mismatched top. It is this festive ensemble that keeps water away from your body. Oh, we never bathe during Stinky Pyjama Time. We never shave our legs. And if you're in SPT long enough, you can actually get the hair on your legs to start doing that giant kelp action in the tub.

Two weeks. Two weeks go by, and every day, I walk up and down the hall, crying, smoking cigarette after cigarette, cradling a little bottle of bourbon like it's a teddy bear. Sometimes, the phone would ring. I would answer it, but before I could talk I'd have to cough up a big hairball so the words could come out.

"Hello? Oh, hi, Maria... No, no, man, I can't go out. I gotta finish this bottle of bourbon... Oh, yeah?... Yeah?... Where did you see him?... Oh, you had a party? At your house?... I didn't know you were having a party... Oh, yeah?... Maria, did it look like he was with somebody?... Oh, yeah?... Did it look like he'd been crying for two weeks?"

No.

Two weeks went by. One day, I got a note from my liver: "We're leaving."

Now, whenever I want to

take my mind off love lost, I do the laundry. I don't know what it is; I think it's just my need to be clean or to be in the basement communing with trolls. One or the other. Or both.

Now I'm still deep in Stinky Pyjama mode, but the light at the end of the tunnel comes by way of a fresh basket of laundry I've just done.

So, the ironing board goes up. The iron starts getting hot. And I'm rummaging around in the basket... and whose shirt comes out? Frank's.

So I lay it really lovingly on the ironing board, and I think, *Okay, he'll see that this shirt is not at his house, and he'll come here. And he'll come here and he'll see that it's here and that I ironed it, and he'll say, "Oh, Sandra, I should never have left you because you're such a good ironer."*

NEVER! Never, never, ever has a man gone for a woman because of her domestic prowess.

"Oh, Enid. What a shiny floor. I've got such a boner for you."

So I'm at the board and I'm feeling so sad. And I'm crying and crying, and I'm thinking, *It's me. It's because of me. If I were way more excellent, he would never have left. That's it. If I were way more excellent, he would never have left.*

And I have Fantasy Number One:

I get amazing legs. Excellent, excellent legs. The kind of leg that when you point the toe there's a line of muscle that starts up at the hip. You know these legs, because you don't have them.

I have them.

And I'm wearing them to a party.

And I'm wearing just a simple sheath of a dress. And I'm sitting on a chair with my legs stretched out to one side, toe pointed like a Vargas pin-up girl, another natural pose, and I am having a conversation with the most beautiful man I have ever seen in my life. This man is so stunning, so devastatingly beautiful... I mean, this man is so good-looking, the only reason you'd ever throw him out of bed is to fuck him on the floor.

Party doors swing open. Who's standing there? Frank. In a parka. And now we have his point of view. He looks down and sees that the ends of those legs are punctuated by stiletto heels. There's a slow camera pan, just moving lazily up the legs. There's that well-turned ankle— mmm. Look at the round of the calf. Ooh la la, that little knee-cap. And just as the camera starts to travel up the body, before it can reveal who it is— (CLAP!)— I am snapped out.

Now I'm looking on, and the camera pans up to reveal... a honey-coloured blonde woman? It's not even me?

And Frank comes over and he takes her hand and then they go off together.

Back at the board, ironing furiously...

Think of something else! Think of something else...

Fantasy Number Two:

I get a Lamborghini. Yes, I get a Lamborghini Countach. Also, by divine intervention, I'm given the gift of driving a standard. Well, it wouldn't do to have the Lamborghini lurching up the street now, would it? So I'm in the Lamborghini, paddling with my feet. And then I'm slapping the gear shift back and forth, toggling with my hand. I'm driving very smoothly, very expertly, up Frank's street, and he's standing in front of his house, and just as I'm about to apply the brakes— (CLAP!)— I'm snapped out.

As I look on the driver's side, I see it's a man driving, not me. A man with black hair and a pale blue seersucker suit. He stops the Lamborghini and he's a friend of Frank's and he beckons Frank into the Lamborghini and they drive off in my car.

Back at the board, the voice of reason comes back, and asks: "Sandra. Sandra. Why aren't you successful even in your own fantasies?"

Fantasy Number Three.

The Reality Sequence:

Frank falls in love with another woman. Oh, my God. Oh, there she is. She's petite. Little ski-jump tits. But her head is only about the size of an orange. But she's got a ton of hair. A fucking ton of hair.

The next shot, they're sitting across the dining table from one another. There's candles lit, there's wine goblets, there's a floral centrepiece, and he's looking across the table into her good eye.

He extends his hand. She drops her teeny hand into his. He guides her around the dining table, and then towards the bedroom.

"Hey, why don't you follow them, Sandra? You're a sick, twisted masochist."

"Well, okay."

Bedroom doors swing open, heavy pink mist action comin' in. He takes her in his arms. He lays her down on the futon. (Love on a budget, you know.) And there they are: intertwined, caressing, kissing sweetly. And just as they're about to make love, it's the darndest thing. He can't get it up. And she's doing a nice imitation of the Sahara Desert. DRY!

You know, I'm back at the board, and I'm feeling a little better.

The phone rings.

I shuffle over.

"Hello."

(It's Frank.)

"Oh, hello... No, I don't mind you calling... No, I wasn't doing anything, I was just, um... standing... How am I? Oh, I'm *fine*... Couldn't be better... Meet you for coffee?... Yeah, I suppose I could meet you... in fifteen minutes..." (I catch a whiff of myself.) "Make it sixteen... Okay... Bye."

Come on, Sandra, pull yourself together... C'mon. You can do it...

I wanna go because I wanna see him but I don't wanna go because I'm afraid.

No, I'm gonna cry...

No. No. No crying. No crying!

I smell like the east end of a horse going west. I'd love to take a long hot bath and make myself soft and sweet, but all I've got time for is a quick slap and tickle with the facecloth and soap, and I promise myself later to dip and strip my legs.

So I'm out the door, going towards the café, and I'm doing that shuffling, crying shit, you know, where there's heavy snot bubble action. I'm afraid to see him, but then I figure, he can only dump me once. I get to the café, and Frank is already sitting there at our table for two.

He's already ordered coffee. He's very handsome, and he's beckoning for me to join him, so I do.

Now, whenever I think I'm going to cry in public, and I don't want to, I think if I jam my thumbnail into my first finger really hard, this teeny little pain from my finger will offset the agony I am feeling in my entire body. It has never worked. I end up weeping openly in public, and I have a weird little groove in my finger.

So, I sit across from him, and he says, "Hi. Hi. It's really good to see you."

He says, "You know... the last two weeks have been pretty hard on me."

He says, "I don't know what it was, I have a lot to tell you. I just kept being reminded of you at every turn. I was at the bookshop and I saw a book you were looking for and I knew you would love it and... uh... I couldn't call you. And late at night if I couldn't get to sleep, I'd go for a walk and sometimes I'd pass in front of your house and I'd see the light on in the living room and I'd think, maybe if I just looked in the window, I'd get to see her. And, ah... I guess I asked you here 'cause, ah... I've had a lot of time to think and... ah... the truth of it is... that I just missed you so bad. I didn't expect to miss you... and I did. And I know I've got no right to ask, and I know I sound like a jerk, and I know there's a lot of things I have to figure out... but, is there any way you can see past what's happened and maybe give us a second..."

"YES!"

"... chance?"

You know, I like to think I hesitated a milli-second on that.

So we sat and we talked and talked and talked and talked and when the waitress came over, I put my brain on her tray.

We had coffee after coffee after coffee and Frank quickly said, "Listen, do you want to go for a walk?"

And we went out into that near perfect autumn night: clear, stars, crisp, beautiful. We walked and talked and walked and we ended up in front of my house.

"Gee, Frank, you know... do you feel like coming in and having a coffee?"

Yeah, that's it. I'll give him renal damage.

So, we both go into the house and it's incredibly awkward. A remarkably awkward moment: we're standing in the living room and we both have our coats on.

So Frank says, in an effort to break the ice, "Why don't we see what's on TV?"

"Yeah, that's a great idea."

And we both reach down for the converter at the very same time, and our hands touch, and there's like this arc of electricity.

Frank says, "THE LAST ONE TO THE BEDROOM'S A DIRTY ROTTEN EGG!"

Naked bodies goin' this way. Coats goin' that way. We run into the bedroom and do a skating stop at the bed... 'cause we're Canadians.

And the bed has fresh sheets.

I just did the laundry.

Sometimes, God says "Yes."

So he stayed the night and we made wild, amazing, wea-sel-like love.

The next morning he had an early call, and he was gone at about seven. So I was alone in bed, and I was in that warm, rosy glow that only women really know. And I was far away from the cuddle puddle. And I was so happy that my boyfriend was back.

(Yay! Yay!)

And I sat up in bed to start my day, and I just happened to look down on the floor. And there, there in the corner of the bedroom, on the floor, was his dirty underwear.

And I thought to myself, *Oh, I get it. My boyfriend's back, and there's gonna be laundry.*

*My Boyfriend's Back and There's
Gonna Be Laundry II:
The Cycle Continues*

Welcome to the second show.

We start the evening off with a performance art piece. This one is entitled, "The Evolution of Men's Underwear." Quickly now, a recap.

Right off the top, huge, nuclear-resistant elastic. Actually, these are the original pair of "show underwear," and they've never been worn. Look what good shape they are in. See what happens when nobody touches them?

Next, the leg area, still boasting that cotton ribbing action.

The opening— the pocket...

The basket area.

All right, the next generation of men's underwear. They're sportier, and streamlined— for the man on the go. Same nuclear-resistant elastic off the top. And the leg area still boasts that cotton ribbing action. But the leg area is just fuckin' huge! I guess, by now, they've figured out men walk, and why not let them?

Next, the opening— the pocket— has been incorporated into a fashion detail, and it just looks like another seam, so you can slip your hand surreptitiously in and out, or just leave it resting in there, sporting a Napoleon Bonaparte look.

Last, and certainly not least, the basket. I'd like to point out that this basket now boasts a little dart, so the material bumps up, and they kinda stick out all by themselves.

And finally, the Ferrari of men's underwear, and the elastic is a full three inches wide. Look at that sucker! I mean, what are you guys afraid of anyway? Your fan belt can only go so many times. Now, the pocket is gone, because we know it is redundant. They've cropped these babies down to just elastic and basket. And look at the size of this basket! Fuck, isn't it the biggest basket you ever saw in your life? I'd like to point out that genetics has not kept up. Man, I could wear these, and just put a yam down there. However, all underwear have one thing in common.

They all look exactly the same balled up on the floor.

Thank you.

Now because this is the second show,

and I wanted to demonstrate a little maturity, I started buying *Lear's* magazine. Now, *Lear's* magazine has since come and gone. But in its hey-day, *Lear's* magazine was published by an organization that thought there was a real dearth of magazines for older women. And to that end, *Lear's* magazine had written, right on their spine:

"For the woman who wasn't born yesterday."

That's me.

So I thought I'd buy this magazine and look into it, because I was not born yesterday. So I put it on the table, crack it open, and there it is on the first two pages: a full-colour, glossy ad for Anti-Wrinkle Cream. Yeah... we don't care if you weren't born yesterday, just don't look it!

And they had this same ad on television, with this very same woman selling this very same product. Okay, the first shot we see is of the woman from the side, and she's ultra-thin, and they've wrapped her head in a towel in a way I have never been able to wrap my head in a towel. You know that little corner piece that you always get hanging down in front of your face? Well, they've managed to make it into a rosette. How darling. I don't know how they did that. Anyway, she's standing there bare-shouldered— wrapped in a towel— and she's got this jar of Anti-Wrinkle Cream in her hand, and the lid is off, and the cream is arranged with a Dairy Queen curl on the top of it, and she delicately dabs the tip of her finger into the curl. Okay. *Nobody* does that. Everybody just scoops it out with their whole hand. And then she dabs it... boop boop boop... in a T-shape on her face. No woman does that. No woman on the planet does that. We lather it up between our palms and slap it on and spread it— whole hand— over the whole area. What's left over, we rub on our hands.

And then we hear a man's voice with a heavy European accent— I think it's Alberto's brother— and he says, "You know, this tiny little jar, it helps to stop the aging process."

This tiny little jar doesn't help to stop the aging process.

A bullet stops the aging process.

Now, there was an ad for Dove... Dove did this ad in an effort to speak to all of us. And you know they're always trying to find real people to sell their products. Commercials "vérité." So they find a woman, and her name is Bev. We see Bev, and Bev says:

"You know, the other day my daughter's boyfriend came over for supper, and he said to me, 'Gosh, Bev, you've got such soft-looking skin.'"

Then Bev says something really weird. She says, "Oh, now, go on with you... it must be the reflection off my sweater."

Now, we see Bev again, and she's standing in her own home, and she's reflected in her foyer mirror, smoothing her hands over her face, and she says, "You know, since I started using Dove, my skin is so soft." Now, we don't see Bev again, but we hear her voice while they're showing us the product, and Bev says,

"You know, Dove has made my skin so soft. Now, if I could just lose twenty pounds."

Oh, fuck off, Bev! Has using the soap made your brain soft?

She's a Mom, she's over forty, and she still can't take a compliment.

"Ah, c'mon, Bev, you've got good skin."

"Oh, sure... but I've got a big wobbly ass!"

You want to lose twenty pounds quick, Bev? Cut off your fuckin' head, you're not using it!

I want to know what's wrong with having wrinkles? What's wrong? Follow along with your own faces. Okay, you see these lines here, these very deep lines I have in my face around my mouth? I got these lines from laughing. I hope you have deep lines in your face from laughing. And I hope they only get deeper. And see these lines here at the sides of my eyes? Crows' feet, I think they're called? I got these lines from probably wincing and saying,

"You want me to suck *what*?"

And this one here, this very deep line right in the middle of my forehead, probably means I had a thought in my head once. So, what can we say about a face that's been stretched into a featureless terrain?

And you know, men aren't

better represented on television. Oh, no, you guys are not! How many men here would wake up their wives or lovers in the middle of the night if their hemorrhoids were giving them trouble?

There's an ad that opens with a guy shaking his wife, going, "Honey! Honey! Wake up!"

"Oh, what is it, sweetheart? Is it your pesky hemorrhoid again? Here, why don't you scratch it with the alarm clock?"

What the fuck do you want me to do about it? Scratch your own ass, God damn it!

Then there was an ad for Robitussin, where this Mom gets really sick, and she's lying in bed, and her husband and her two large sons are standing over her, looking at her, and she brings the covers up, and says,

"Oh, don't get too close, you might get my cold."

And the youngest one cries out, "Who's gonna take care of us now that Mom's sick?"

Well, you're going to die, you little fucker, 'cause your dad can't boil an egg!

Next!

Okay, now there was an ad a while ago, and this was one of those ads where they reversed the roles, but it does none of us justice, not one of us. This one is for dishwasher detergent. The premise of this ad is that three men have invited three women over for dinner. The table is immaculately set, there's china, there's crystal, there's a centrepiece, there's the whole nine yards. And the women are just sitting there, doing dick. The three guys are in the kitchen, and one of them turns around with a silver platter in his hands, and proudly says,

"Voilà! Speckled trout à la Mike!"

and one of his guests picks up a wine glass, holds it up to the light, and says,

"Well, I guess that's not all that's speckled!"

Have you lost your fuckin' mind? These guys have *plates*. No man ever invited me over to his home for speckled trout.

Trouser trout, yeah...

And I do not remember a silver platter presentation.

Welcome now

to the Wild Wild World of Women. Da da da da da da da da...
I *always* hear sports music for this.

Now, when I turned thirty years old, I went to the doctor's
for my five-year–fifty-thousand mile check-up. It was different
from when I was twenty-nine, because you know, when you're
twenty-nine, you go in— quick, pap, pulse— and you're out
of there. I turned thirty, and I went to the doctor's, and she
said, "Well, now that you're thirty, you'll be subjected to adult
testing." And to that end, they started wheeling in these stainless
steel dim sum carts.

It's the same for everybody: you go in and you remove your
clothes. You are buck-naked under fluorescent lights— which
is really the most diplomatic lighting in the world, don't you
think? There's like a piece of Kleenex with a hole in it to wear,
and you pop that over your head. Now it goes just below your
tits. You're naked. Oh, but you've got a lovely bib on.

Jump on the examination table; put your feet in the oven
mitts— my doctor covers her stirrups with oven mitts. Then,
you skrinch your bum down to the end of the examination
table— because you know she'll ask— and wait in this attractive, comfortable position until the doctor comes in.

She enters rubbing her hands vigorously and says, "Okay,
now! Let's get started, shall we?" First, it's once around the

breasts to check for lumps, a quick squeeze of each nipple—
then we're on to the manual examination of the pelvis. Then,
just when you are having too much fun, she says, "Now you
just lie still while I go get the speculum."

Where does the speculum live, Canada? Right next to the
Häagen-Dazs!

She comes back, she's cranking that fucker open, and it's
smoking! After the exam, she says, "You know, Sandra, you've
been on the pill a long time."

"I had expressed an interest in changing contraceptives, but
as you know, the pill is *really* convenient."

She says, "Maybe you just want to go off it for a while, to
give your body a rest."

"Ah, no, c'mon!!! No! Finally I'm getting laid regularly and
I've got to go off the pill?"

I did inquire about a retroactive clause for all the years I was
taking it for nothing.

So I asked her:

"What are my fashion choices?"

Right off the top, IUD.

Inter-Uterine Device. Well, we take from the name,
"IUD," that it goes in the uterus, and it does. But... it doesn't
like to stay there. No, it's a wandering IUD. It travels around
in your body. Forty ultrasounds later, "Oh, there it is, Sandra!
It's in your wrist!"

Diaphragm. Stretched out big enough, it's perfect for
catching people falling out of burning buildings.

And finally, condoms and foam.

Condoms and foam. My partner and I, well, we're nineties people... you know... and since it's *our* penis—

My period.

Our penis.

— we decided to use condoms and foam. And so I went to the drugstore and I bought condoms and I *was* gonna buy foam. But they had a huge display of foam, and I ran my finger along one of the boxes, and there was dust on it. And I thought, *If nobody else is buying it, neither am I!* We'll just use several extra condoms.

It's very hard to change contraception methods. The pill is *really* convenient, and I mean you don't really know what it's doing to you until a nice third arm grows out of the middle of your chest.

So, it was difficult, and there was all this stuff around condoms. First of all, condoms come in little boxes, and on the front there's always a man and a woman, they're standing holding hands in a tidal pool, and the sun is setting behind them. These people don't need condoms. They need a map. They are lost.

Next, it is considered a mutually loving thing if you help your guy on with the condom. But there are so many obstacles, really. You snap the box open and you take them all out. Sometimes they're all slung together like a little accordion.

Don't play around with that too much; you don't look sincere.

Just snap one of those babies off and wait around... for an erection, I guess. Now, there is a statute of limitations governing how long you can effectively apply a condom, and this is made more difficult by the fact that some of the packages don't have a "starter" nick like take-out ketchup has. That little nick could help you along when you need it the most.

So, ping, one erect penis!

"Hang on, honey! I'll be right there, just hold on."

So you're hot, sweaty, and naked, and you're trying to open this slippery little plastic package. You have no choice. You have to use your teeth to chew it open. That's attractive. And if that doesn't fucking scare him, then you have to shove this thing on somehow. And when it's finally on, it always looks so painful.

"Is it on? Can you breathe with that thing on?"

Quickly, now: Condoms of Interest. A condom update.

When condoms became everyday items, they started manufacturing different kinds. Now you can get a squidgillion different kinds. One of the very first ones they came out with was a Rameses condom that they touted as twenty per cent larger. Their marketing reasoning for this was,

"Well, we feel men would be more comfortable with a roomier condom."

Well, let's face it, who would ever buy a smaller one? And what was the name of that little gem? *Magnum*! So the next time you sleep with a man and he puts on a condom and it's hangin' off his dick, you can save the situation, and say,

"Hey!!! That'd make a great windsock, wouldn't it?"

Now there was this other condom— you know these ones— they glow in the dark. Apparently it's not like wearing a mining helmet to bed, but the condom itself *will* emit a soft glow for up to five hours. All right. And I thought, *Why do I want to know where the garbage can is for four and a half hours?* But they'd be great for nudist night camping.

Trojan came out with these ads a while ago. Basically, they used fear as a motivator for everybody to get the idea that you *must* use a condom. It's just about saving your life now, and I guess they wanted to scare you to death before you went out and fucked yourself to death. Trojan had a series of ads, and they were really weird, kind of dark and macabre. I remember one... You see the wheelbase of a vehicle, and then you see the tires and the car going really fast. Originally, I thought this was a Gravol commercial. So the car's going faster and faster and faster and faster, and then you hear squealing tires, smashing glass, bending metal, and you hear The Voice of Doom say:

"Before things get out of control: Trojan condoms!"

Start screaming now!

So I thought, *Now, how could they sell everybody a condom, rise up to everybody's intelligence and sell condoms right across the board?* And I thought, *Why doesn't Michelin make them?* They could have copy like,

"Yes, these wide-treaded babies get you in and out of places you never thought you'd go!"

They could have Bib, the Michelin Man, that big white blubbery thing? What the fuck is that, anyway? He's always seen waving hello, so he's got a free hand that he could point at his rubber dick...

When I was a little girl,

I wondered how women knew how to do things. How did women know how to make all the food for a meal ready at the same time? This point is best exemplified if you've ever been invited over to a man's house for dinner, and you're sitting in the living room, and he comes out with a bowl and says,

"These are ready. Would you like one of these?"

"I'd love a Brussels sprout. Thank you."

So I started watching women to try to discover how they knew how to do things. I started watching women to see how they chose a stall in a public washroom. Now, I have seen women walk into a public washroom and glide by all the stalls, like they're feeling for the right one.

"No... No... No... No... Oh, yeah. This is it. This is *mine*."

Now the first thing you do when you go into the stall is lock the door. If it doesn't have a lock on it, move on. Because if it doesn't have a lock on it, then you have to pee bent at the waist in the pike position, with your arms stuck out straight out, trying to hold the door closed.

Next, don't leave your purse on the floor. I always think there's a bogeyman in the bathroom with a hook and he'll scoop your purse away. There's a knob at the top of the door. That's where you put your purse. On the knob.

And last, but before anything happens, the voice of every woman who ever took you to the bathroom in your whole entire life comes forward and you hear:

"Don't sit! Don't you sit! You'll get bum cancer!"

So women have invented these amazing hovering techniques. Some women actually take the time out of their busy day to wrap the entire toilet seat with toilet paper. And you know who you are! The first time I saw that I said,

"Oh, my God! It's a nest!"

I sit.

I'm a pig.

Now, there's really not much to do in there. The environment is fairly job-specific. Except that sometimes, there's graffiti. Women write graffiti on the walls. But way more fascinating to me is that women carry magic-markers in their purses. 'Cause you don't go into a bathroom and there's a long string with a magic-marker hanging on it.

"Oh, maybe I'll just leave my shortbread recipe on here."

So here's some of the best graffiti I've ever seen in my whole life. Sometimes, written at the bottom of the door in extended-arm scrawl is:

"Beware the limbo walker."

If that's there, I just lift my feet off the floor.

And then there's this, and you really know how she was feeling when she wrote this:

"It starts when you sink into his arms, and ends with your arms in his sink."

And then there's graffiti that women respond to. They answer one another back... no, not that bitch who goes around writing:

"Spelling!" in a circle with an arrow.

Get a fuckin' life!

One woman wrote, "My mother made me a lesbian." And another woman responded, "If I give her the wool, will she make me one, too?"

So, you're sitting there. There's a woman next to you, and she has shoes on. That's a good sign. Inevitably, in your public peeing career, you will hear,

"Excuse me? Is there any toilet paper in your stall?"

The unwritten rule amongst women is that you never go... "Maybe."

If you've got it, you *must* share! It's the law! Next, how much? How much? What's a regular serving of toilet paper? The figures differ amazingly on this. I asked an audience once, "How much?", and a man yelled out, "Four times around the hand!" He's got time. I mean he must have it down to a science, because you know how much men are fascinated by the amount of toilet paper women use. They say things like, "What the hell are you doing with it?"

"I'm trading it to the Gypsies for whiskey. What the hell do you *think* I'm doing with it?"

Now, even before you hand her the toilet paper, the dispensers will give you trouble. If the roll is on too tight, you have to unroll it by hand, working up a proper sweat.

Then there's this other dispenser— and if you've ever seen it— don't leave me alone on this— the inside bar is black oval plastic, and the mechanism that it's on allows it to turn only a quarter-turn. Do you know this fuckin' evil thing? So when you pull the paper, it pulls it back! In order to get paper, you have to roll it around your fingers, shove it backwards along the roll, and reach around underneath to grab it.

Repeat forty times.

"Fuck off!"

And finally, those silver metal boxes. Sanitation for the Nation. What comes out, Canada? Waxed paper, but with a serrated edge. This stuff has the traction of teflon and the absorbency of zinc. Don't use it. You'll get a paper cut that will never heal!

Okay, now if everything's going well, I'll do my usual serving— two pulls' worth across the body— and then I cut it. I figure that amount covers all the bases. Now you don't want this woman to think you're a pig, so fold it nice. Take your time. She's not going anywhere. Now you're bent at the waist and hunkered down for the pass. And she's got her little hand twisted backward, fingers pointed up, under the stall wall. You drop it in her hand, and you always hear a big sigh, "Oh, thank you!"

You have done a good thing. God knows how long she was there. This one time I passed the paper, and I heard the woman say, "Well! I certainly don't need *this* much!" Hey, what are you, a dabber? Use it all, make like it's your birthday.

All right, you're outta there. Flush with your foot.

Now... you don't have to wash your hands if there's nobody else at the sink. But if you actually go by and don't wash your hands and there's a woman at the sink, you're busted. She'll give you that look in the mirror: *Unclean!* So, I rinse my hands. I play with the water. But I've seen women stand at the sink and scrub like surgeons. And I'd love to say,

"Excuse me, you wouldn't have to do that if you used paper."

I'm on my way out of this washroom, and there, on the side of the condom machine, some remarkable woman has written in green magic-marker, "This is the weirdest gum I ever chewed."

When I was in my early twenties,

a lot of the young women I knew actually planned to have children, like they knew even at a very very young age that they were going to have children.

"Oh, yeah, for sure, for sure I'm gonna have a ton of kids. Oh, yeah!"

Now, you see, I didn't understand this at all, because at that time I was developing a cross-addiction between drugs and alcohol, so I was very busy this whole time. I didn't know what they were talking about... The calling? The Voice?

I'm suckin' on a joint, thinking, *Yeah, I think I hear the voice, now, yeah!*

So I went very numbly through most of those years and I really did believe that I would be immune to that biological clock shit.

I'll never forget the day it happened. I was standing in the eight-or-less-item check-out at Dominion. Don't ever, ever stand in front of me with eleven items. Not unless you'd like to eat three right there.

So I'm standing there, I've got two frozen orange juices in my hand, and I'm waiting in line. There's a young Mom in front of me, and there's a baby in the stroller, and she's all in pink fuzzy Borg. She's a riot of pink fuzzy Borg, and she has on one of those white angora hats with the little ears. God, she's cute.

I'm looking at this little sweet face and I'm standing there thinking, *My God, don't they package them beautifully?*

Then, I hear The Voice. The Voice that comes from your crotch.

"*Baby.*"

"Uh-huh... baby... Hey, sweetheart. Hi."

"*Isn't it a cute baby?*"

"Yeah, it really is a sweet baby."

"*Why don't you go home and have a baby?*"

"Oh, what a great idea!"

It was so strong, I felt like I was being led around by the uterus. It was so weird. I didn't tell anybody, 'cause when you've done as many drugs as I have, you don't tell people you heard a voice coming out of your crotch at the check-out in Dominion!

Then things started happening to aid and abet pregnancy. Like, one day I finally found my dial-pack of birth control pills. I blew the dust off it and looked at it, and it seems that I'd missed six pills. Uh-oh. I just ate the whole pack. Mm-mmm good.

And I'd be walking, or I'd be in an elevator, and I'd see a pregnant woman, and I'd get closer to her.

You know how pregnant women are constantly complaining about those lunatics who stare at them? I was one of them, for God's sakes!

And it didn't come close until my best friend Sherry got pregnant. She and her husband, Bill, decided to start their family, and Sherry got pregnant to help out.

She was over at my house one day because we were going to make her some maternity clothes. When we went shopping for maternity clothes, it was amazing: I mean, garments with little Peter Pan collars and colours not found in nature. I'm thinking, *You're just pregnant, you're not stupid, for God's sakes.* So we're laying out the pattern and we've got the material, and she catches me staring at her stomach.

I go, "Sherry, can I please see your belly bare naked?"

And she went, "Oh, yeah, sure!"

So we ran upstairs to the bedroom and she pulls her top off. I remember: Okay, okay... big... big... very white... big white... big! big... her stomach... Big... and her tits started under her armpits somewhere, I don't even know where. And her belly just went out went out went out, and it was totally covered with skin. And her belly button had just gone out one day and never came back. You could hang your keys on it. And hard, hard. I was forced to head-butt it. And she didn't even budge!

I said, "Sherry, tell me about being pregnant. I hear you get sick in the beginning."

"Well, you know, it's more like three months."

"So, you get sick a couple of times in the first three months?"

"No... you *puke* for three *months.*"

I thought, *Oh, man! Who's going to hold my hair?*

And she went on and on and on and on. I stuck my fingers in my ears and hummed the national anthem. It was more than I needed to know.

Sherry had a very healthy pregnancy, thank you for asking. And one day, while she was shopping, she went into labour. Yes! I hope I go down shopping, man! And she gave birth to a little baby girl named Sadie. She was just a little piece of pie.

She was so sweet I could just eat her. So I went to visit Sherry in the hospital, and she looked tired, you know.

I said, "Gosh, hon, you look a bit tired."

And she growled, "You'd look fuckin' tired, too!"

Sherry had been in labour for twenty-seven hours. *I* have never done *anything* for twenty-seven hours, let alone wait around for a television set to fall out of my body!

"Sherry? Sherry, hon... did it... hurt?"

She gave me a what-the-fuck-do-you-think look.

"Sherry, you know those women who say, 'Oh, sure it hurt, but you forget all about the pain when you see the baby?' Sherry, have you forgotten about the pain?"

She shook her head. Big *NO*.

My fascination with Sherry's pregnancy was a real departure for me, because I was always the one who hit my knees nightly and prayed the Single Girl's Prayer. Pray along if you know the words:

"Dear God, dear God, please, please give me my period. Please give me my period and I'll never do it again!"

The house that I was born and

raised in, in Sudbury, Ontario, was on the Trans-Canada Highway.

The Trans-Canada Highway goes right across Canada. Hence the name.

And when I was growing up in Sudbury, this highway went right through the city. Of course, now they've built a bypass around the city, and why wouldn't they? More recently, Sudbury has become known because it's the centre for the Taxation Department. Did you know this? Of course you do.

Anyway, I am five years old. It is a sunny, summer Sunday in Sudbury. I am standing on the sidewalk, spending some quality time with my Dad. We are standing on the sidewalk in front of our house, watching the cars on the Trans-Canada. That's how it went. My Dad was a mechanic, and he liked to watch the cars go by. He'd amuse himself by noticing foreign plates.

"Oh, Michigan, yup." He rocks on his heels.

So I'm standing there with my Dad, and he's using his thumb as a pointer, and he says to me, "Sandra, you see this way here? This is east. Now, if you walk as far as you can go, east, you'll get to St. John's, Newfoundland."

Jingle jingle jingle... The change in his pocket.

"And this way here, that's west. Now, if you walk as far as you... Sandra! Sandra, come back here! If you walk as far as you can go, west, you'll get to Vancouver, British Columbia. And that's lovely any time of year."

Jingle jingle jingle...

My Dad was the kind of Dad who would spend an entire afternoon trying to explain the magic of magnets. Holding up two seemingly inert pieces of metal, he would say,

"Now, you see, there's a north pole and a south pole, and when the poles are opposite they attract."

And he would push the pieces of metal together.

"But when they're the same, then they repel, do you see that?"

No, okay, you can't *see* magnetism, you have to experience it, and he would never let me hold them. So for all I fuckin' knew he was just pushing them together and then pulling them apart. I didn't know.

My Mom fancied herself a self-made hair stylist.

One day, when everything was buffed and baked, she decided that *I* should have bangs.

Now, I have naturally curly hair, and it's like cheesies on my head. My mother decided that this hair should lay neatly on what little forehead I have.

I'm in the kitchen, sitting on the stepstool, and I've got the shower curtain wrapped around my neck, with a clothespin holding it tight. She goes and gets the comb, the family comb. It is a yellow, rat-tail comb. She runs it under the water, makes a part, and combs my hair. She wets and combs and wets and combs and wets and combs my bangs... and when you wet and comb curly hair, it doesn't go down. It just makes one big curl swooping up.

She goes to the drawer and gets the good scissors— after all, I am her daughter— and she starts at one side at eyebrow level and goes to the middle of my forehead.

Cut... cut cut.

She's about to start from the other side when the phone rings.

"Hello..."

"*Ah, ya allah...!*" It's my aunt.

Now my mother and my aunt are locked at the mouth.

And I'm still sitting on the stepstool, water just evaporating off my forehead— it's a simple scientific fact that when curly hair dries, it shrinks.

She's off the phone, some forty minutes later.

She sees that she's only got half the job done.

"I'll just finish it off," she reasons.

Cut... cut... cut...

"Okay. It's too long."

Cut cut cut.

"Oops, too short.

Panic. "Okay, okay, okay."

And she cuts one more time in an effort to make it even.

I have what is called a widow's peak. After my beauty session in the kitchen, I had a "widow's bang" around it. Man, I was ugly. I looked like a geek. I was fucking ugly and I knew it.

Don't think children don't know.

Children know.

So rather than add insult to injury, I would only view my new hair-do in the toaster. We had a chrome, Sunbeam toaster with a convex face, and it was like looking into a funhouse mirror. It did not give a good representation of reality. Even as a child, I knew reality was something to escape.

My Mother had her own medical thing going;

she had her own medicine, you know?

My Mother would say things like, "Eat onions, they have oxygen in them."

Try to imagine my surprise the first time I see Jacques Cousteau at the bottom of the ocean without a big bag of Bermudas.

She also thought that tobacco smoke possessed a medicinal property. When I was little, whenever I would get an earache, my Mother would go to the medicine cabinet and take out a pack of Black Cat cigarettes, light one cigarette, and say, "Come here."

And you go. You go, because... she's your Mom.

You don't go, "No! You're a fuckin' maniac! Look what you did to my hair!"

You go.

And she takes a drag of the cigarette, bends down, cups her hands around my ear, and blows smoke in my ear. I never did benefit. I just got a big yellow ear.

I was an only child for six years.

Six of the most beautiful years of my life. And then one day it looked like my Mom had swallowed the Marconi television set.

Yes, she was great with child. And on a very hot, blisteringly hot, June 21st, 1963, my brother Michael was born.

All my ancient aunts were crying, "Oh, thanks to God! Oh, it's a boy! It's a boy! He'll carry the name!"

"Where's the name gotta go, Grandma? Maybe I can take it."

So my mother brings the little pudge ball home, and all the adults are ringed around the layette, with that freshly loboto-mized look, staring at the beautiful child. I push my way through the throng, going, "Excuse me, excuse me..."

Looking over the rim of the bassinette, I say, "Hmph. I don't see nothing special about him."

I get a slap in the head.

That's the day I became a feminist.

Not because he was a boy, but because suddenly I was frozen shit on a stick.

He went on to have a stellar career as a child. Oh, yeah.

He got an orange banana seat bike with high handlebars and streamers. I did not. And my Mom never cut *his* hair.

One day, he was lying on my Mom's bed, and she's changing his diaper, and he's bare naked. Babies love to be bare naked. She says to me,

"Sandra, I have to go and get a washcloth. Watch your brother."

"Well, okay..."

So I'm standing there, watching my brother. And before my very eyes, his little penis goes up, and he pees a perfect arc from my Mom's bed into his own crib. For a six-year-old, that's high humour, and I collapsed laughing. I thought, *Well, he might be a waste of skin, but he can do this one excellent trick!*

Michael graduated to baby apparatus number one: a jolly jumper. A jolly jumper's just a canvas seat hung from chains that go into a rubber tube that screws into a doorway or an arch. You just slam the baby into that and the baby hangs there, bobbing. Tons of fun, eh?

"Sandra, I have to start supper. Watch your brother."

So I'm standing there, watching my brother. I push down on his head, and he bobs straight up. Hey! I push down harder and he bobs up higher. I pull him back like a rock in a slingshot and let go. He bobs horizontally between two rooms for about ten seconds. I'm amazed. Then, he starts screaming.

My mother comes running into the room. "What's wrong with your brother?"

"I don't know," I say innocently. "He does look a little peakèd, though. Maybe you should blow smoke in his ear."

So Michael graduated to baby apparatus number two: a walker. Michael's walker was a square metal frame, and it had four wheels on it, and there was a piece of blue canvas slung in it for the baby to sit on, and in the front there were beads. Why? Maybe if the baby's head lolled forward, he could count with his tongue.

My mother said, "You know, it's a beautiful day outside. Why don't we put the baby outside, in his walker?"

Where do we live?

And she says to me, "Sandra. Watch your brother."

And I never took my eyes off that child. I watched him the

whole time. And I should say that Michael was excellent at walker.

I watched him the whole time. I watched him go down onto the driveway. I watched him. I watched him go all the way down the driveway, I watched him hit the sidewalk, and then I watched as he turned towards Vancouver. He was making excellent time. He's past Mrs. Dionne's house already, and he's past Mrs. Solosky's driveway, the bus stop's behind him, and he's almost at Burt's Confectionery. No one's allowed to go to Burt's Confectionery. I don't even think my Dad went as far as Burt's Confectionery. It was the edge of the earth.

My mother comes around the corner of the house with the garden hose in her hand, stops dead, and does that maternal radar thing... No baby!

She pales. "Where's your brother!?"

"Um, see that little bobbing thing there? That's Mike."

She comes toward me, thinking, *No, I can't kill her yet.* "GO GET YOUR BROTHER! RUN!"

So I run like a girl all the way down the street, and by this time Mike's hooked on a curb. Oh, and he's mad. He's mad. He's not used to not getting things his way. He's mad. So I pull him off the curb and set him straight and I think, *Oh, man, I'm going back for the biggest beating of my life.* "What do you say, Mike? What do you say, you drive? We'll go to Vancouver. I'll get a job." No dice. I drag him back, screaming, and I can see my mother standing there, sharpening her hand.

My parents were married through an arranged marriage. Yes, an arranged marriage. They didn't like each other then and they never got to like each other. No, these two people weren't even good neighbours. And they spent the bulk of their free time thinking of new and inventive ways to be fucking evil to each other! So the house was either a screaming bedlam, or we were plunged into silence. That kind of silence that has weight.

So some fifteen years later, my parents decided to divorce.

"What took you so long? You didn't stay together for us, did you?" Because look at us. We're damaged. We all came out of our parents' marriage and their subsequent divorce with exactly the same thinking— my brother, my sister, and my-self— we were never, ever, ever going to get married. And we were never going to have children. Seen marriage, didn't care for it. Thank you, no. Why would I ever get married when I could just put a hot wire in my eye?

So this role model that my parents presented to us was unsuitable, I have to say. And so, I decided to become a career woman. Yes, I was going to become a career woman, and I was going to have wind blowing in my hair the whole time. Even when I was a little kid, even when I was a child, I always knew what I wanted to be when I grew up.

I wanted to be an archaeologist.

Well, am I?

It is the first day of grade nine.

I am resplendent in a hot-pant outfit my mother has made me. I am called down to the Guidance Counsellor's office for guidance and counselling. My Guidance Counsellor was the oldest member of the teaching staff there at that time. She was the Latin teacher, probably because that was her first language. So I go into the room, and there, crumpled behind a massive oak desk, was this ancient woman.

"Now, Sandra... " she croaks, "what would you like to do with the rest of your life, dear?" Her tongue was lolling around in her mouth.

"I'd like very much to be an archaeologist."

"Oh, lord! That's no work for a girl."

I didn't know I was a girl.

I didn't know that because I was a girl, there were things I wasn't supposed to do.

I didn't know that my tits were career-blockers.

So the minute I could, I left school, because there was nothing for me there, and I left home at the very same time, because there was certainly nothing for me there. And I found gainful employment at the Bamboo Gardens, The Home of Fine Canadian and Chinese Cuisine. During this time, I had met a fascinating woman by the name of Louise Tranche-Montagne.

First of all, Louise represented to me a kind of woman who demonstrated tremendous independence, and she had an invulnerability that I admired. She was unlike any woman I'd ever met up until that point.

Of course, at the point that I knew Louise, she had never

married, but that was fine, that was part of who Louise was. She lived with her folks, and that was fine, because that was all part of Louise.

I was asking Louise for some advice, and she said, "Let me tell you, eh? Dere are two t'ings to remember. Don't wear your 'eart on your sleeve, eh? And always, always 'ave your own money. Dat way you don't owe nobody not'ing, eh?"

You see, Louise had a bit of a cottage-craft industry. Louise manufactured Bingo Marker Cans. Now, I know what you're thinking: *Sandra, there's no call for those here in Toronto.* Well, I agree with you, but they go like hotcakes in Sudbury. This was, of course, before the bingo dabber technology. They just took the art right out of bingo.

So Louise continued, and said, "'Ave your own money, eh? Dat's why I make de Can. To make de Can, you get a nice tobacco tin, a nice one— make sure dere's no tobacco inside. Next, get a nail, eh, comme ça, and poke a hole all the way around the top of the can. Poke poke poke poke. Voilà! Next, go to de K-Mart, uh? And buy de same colour Phentex as de can. De Export tin, uh, dey are green, eh? Buy de same colour as de can. Dey don't always 'ave it, eh? Get de Phentex and put it in de 'ole all de way around de top of de can, and make de loop. Den, get a nice crochet hook and crochet a nice mesh all de way around de top of de can, den put de Phentex to be de drawstring, eh?

"Sometime, when I'm feeling fancy, I put de pom-pom. Open de top of de mesh, pour your bingo marker inside, and close it up nice. Voilà! Bingo Marker Can. My brother, Claude, he's a priest, eh? He can bless de whole shebang for you."

Now, it was around this time

that I decided I should try my hand at relationships.

I knew nothing of love. Where would I have learned about it? But apparently, you could have this *other* thing called a successful relationship and the idea of love didn't even seem to enter into it. I was reading *Cosmo*, and it had one of those quizzes in it. And you'd answer these questions, and how you answered them determined whether or not you had a successful relationship. Answers to questions like, you know:

Do you share?

Do you communicate?

Have you lost your gag reflex?

Stuff like that. These are all instrumental to a successful relationship.

So I went out into the world. Now, I thought if you just stayed with the same person for an inordinate length of time, for almost no reason at all, *that* was a successful relationship. Oh, but it's not; it's boredom.

Then I moved on. Oh, I thought if you changed yourself entirely to meet somebody else's expectations... and I'm sure I'm the only one who's ever done that... I thought *that* was a successful relationship. But it's not; it's stupidity.

And then I thought, if you got somebody, hollowed them out and put what you wanted into them— oh, *that* was a successful relationship! But it's not. It's boredom *and* stupidity.

Luckily, at the time, I was cross-addicted to drugs and alcohol, so I was just having the time of my life.

It is February 17, 1986.

I'm living in Toronto. The phone rings. It is my sister, Tannia, calling.

Tannia says, "Sandra, Dad died. He died tonight at eight o'clock."

And I looked at my watch and it was ten minutes after eight, and my Dad had been dead for ten minutes and my Dad was going to be dead for the rest of my life. When my head heard the news, I went "Thank God," because my Dad had lived a long and loveless life and had experienced tremendous pain and now that he was dead he was never ever going to have to feel pain ever again. And that was really a cause to celebrate. But when my heart heard it, I went into shock, and I said to Tannia, "Are you sure?"

And Tannia said, "Oh, yeah, I'm pretty sure. He didn't stand up when I came in the room."

You know, we're on the phone; it's like the room is empty but for the phone; it's really a fuckin' evil instrument sometimes. So I'm wandering off into shock and I could hear Tannia's voice going, "Sandra, Sandra..."

I go, "What?"

And she says, "They want a suit for Dad."

"What?"

She says, "They want us to pick out a suit for Dad, they want to lay Dad out in a suit."

And I say, "Well, fuck, thank God he's dead!" 'Cause you see, my Dad would have never done it, otherwise. No, my Dad was Plaid Master! He could put plaids together like no man's business. And I said, "Well, Tannia, what've we got? What are our fashion choices?"

She says, "Well, there's the Trudeau suit."

Ah. It's 1967, Centennial year, Canada's birthday. My Dad celebrates by buying a suit. It was an olive-green plaid, single-breasted. The pants had skinny legs and a bit of a flare. And when he wore this suit, he thought he looked like Pierre Elliott Trudeau. And you had to kind of give it to him, too...

"Oh, Mr. Trudeau...

"Oh, it's just Dad! You really had me going!"

And I said, "Well, is that it, Tannia?"

She says, "Well, there's the houndstooth check..."

Hang on! It's 1972, and in a fashion frenzy— for my Dad— he goes out and buys this suit. There was a guy in Sudbury, and he had a men's clothing store called Stu Woodruff's, and he'd do his own ads, and he'd come on TV with only his face showing and go,

"When you walk down the street, only ten percent of you shows. The rest is good clothes. And where do you find those good clothes, my friends?"

My Dad jumps in the car and drives down to Stu Woodruff's. He comes back with the houndstooth check from Hell! It's 1972. The checks on this fucker were a foot square... there's room on the front of that suit for like four whole checks. And the lapels were so wide, they needed runway clearance.

I said, "Well, Tannia, what speaks to you here?"

She says, "I like the houndstooth."

I said, "Then let's go with that... I guess he needs a shirt."

She says, "You know he prefers a short sleeve."

"Okay, booboo, put a short sleeve on him."

And she said, "And I guess, The Tie."

The Tie of Myth and Legend. My Dad's favourite tie went with both suits. It was wide. Wide. My brother always said, "A little wider and a little longer, he wouldn't have needed pants." It had a beige background, neutral background, and then huge, red chrysanthemums on it. He looked like he'd been shot repeatedly in a confined space.

We put our Dad in a suit, and our Dad went to Heaven. Our Dad deserved to go to Heaven. And we were left here to stand on the planet and go to Hell.

I cannot tell you what it is like to lose a parent,
but for the first time in my life I lost my sense of humour. I have never been without my sense of humour. It is my most precious possession, if I can call it that. And when it was gone... I don't know if you've noticed, but to actually live on this planet, you have to have a sense of humour. When mine was gone, man, the world was just coming at me uncensored, and it was too much. I just started shutting down.

I was working at the time as a puppeteer in a show called *Fraggle Rock...* Yeah, I had a real job. I wiggled dolls for Henson. I went back to work, and the people who I worked with wanted very much to express their condolences, but to be near someone who's had death nearby, especially the death of a parent, is to be reminded of your own mortality, certainly the mortality of your parents, so people very generously offered their condolences at arm's length. So there was a lot of air around me.

When I got back to work there was a new puppeteer. This new puppeteer's name was Frank, and nobody was paying much attention to Frank because he was new, and nobody knew what to expect. So one day this guy Frank and I are sharing a wooden box on set. We're sitting back to back, and I was sitting there playing with a piece of thread, which I found incredibly soothing. Suddenly I feel this tap on my shoulder and I look up, and it's this new guy, and he says, "Listen, I just heard about your Dad and I just want to express my condolences."

Very small, "Thank you."

Tap tap tap. "Listen, is there anything I can do?"

"Oh, no, thank you."

Tap tap tap.

"Listen, can I buy you a meal? You know, can I take you out for supper?"

Anytime is suppertime! And the bereaved, they do like to eat, you know.

So this guy, Frank, and I, go to this Hungarian restaurant called The Tarragato. It used to be at the corner of Bathurst and Bloor. It was an excellent, excellent place. All the waitresses at The Tarragato used to wear the official Hungarian waitresses' boot. Do you know this? The official Hungarian waitresses' boot looks like a Roman legionnaire's with the laces up the front, but the toe and the heel are cut out... I'm alone, aren't I? So we're sitting at The Tarragato, in a booth, and it's kinda dimly lit and we're listening to "Hotel California" on the accordion. You really haven't heard it until you've heard it done on the accordion.

I'm sitting there, I have no life in me, I'm just upright, basically, and I order the chicken paprikash.

Now, when you make chicken paprikash, you boil the chicken; you cut up the chicken and you boil it. When you boil chicken with the skin on, the skin kinda goes gross and wobbly. So there's a mound of chicken with gross wobbly skin at one end of a big oval dish, and on the other side there's all these little dumplings. Really fucking belligerent looking dumplings, saying, "C'mon bitch, eat me, I dare ya!" And it's all swimming in an off-red moat of paprika sauce. Basically, I've ordered a meal that looks like I feel. Frank has ordered the schnitzel, and large men bring it in, with a small Husqvarna chain saw. I don't care. I just lower my head to my plate and I start shovelling it off the lip into my mouth.

Frank puts his utensils down for a second and watches me refuel with a little horror, and he says,

"Sandra, I've been thinking about how you must feel with your Dad's passing, and you know, I've never lost a parent, but I know how it feels to be very sad, so if you ever need somebody to talk to, I'd love to be of help to you."

I look across the table incredulously, trying to focus.

I think to myself, *Is this guy trying to relate?*

And he continues and says, "Listen, I'm serious, if you ever need anything, you know, please, please give me a call."

I started to cry. Not a sudden big blast of crying, but a quiet, accumulative kind of crying that rolls down your body and pools around the legs of your chair. I couldn't believe a perfect stranger was extending a compassionate hand. I couldn't believe it was a guy. So I went on crying, that quiet crying, and Frank goes, "Don't cry... please don't cry.... oh, okay, you have to cry... Check! Check! Now would be good! Check, check!"

So, he picks me up, takes me to my house, sits me down on the couch, fluffs up a pillow, puts it behind my back, and puts my legs up on the coffee table.

And then he did something I've never seen any other man do in my life. He took the converter and put it in my hand, and went down the hall to make a pot of coffee. I thought I had entered the portal to an alternative dimension! And, just for a micro-second, I actually viewed this guy with different eyes:

Whoa! Look at the basket on that!

He was true to his word. Every now and then, there'd be a knock at the door. It'd be this guy, Frank, with a little bag, a couple of bran muffins. He'd come in, he'd make a pot of coffee, and we just sat there and ate. I didn't say anything. I had nothing to say.

Eight weeks went by. I counted every day of eight weeks after my father died, and one day I actually laughed out loud. This guy Frank made me laugh. And I would laugh and laugh and laugh. Like, a chucklehead, a chucklehead laugh. Do you know this laugh? Chucklehead is a denomination of laughter. Chucklehead laughing is when stuff flies out of your nose. So this guy Frank would make me laugh until my stomach ached— laugh and laugh— and I would make him laugh, and he loved the fact that I have a sense of humour and he wasn't threatened that I had a sense of humour and that I actually knew how to use it. You see, in my experience, a woman's sense of humour was always gauged by how much *she* would laugh at a man's jokes. So it was so refreshing to meet somebody who encouraged me to make him laugh, and I just I loved that. I made him laugh, and we'd laugh and laugh and laugh and stuff would fly. It was great.

So we'd hang out, we'd go to movies, we'd go to the occasional dinner, or walk, and one day, you know... we started looking at each other, you know, in that way. You know the way, when people are interested in each other's genitals, you know what I'm saying.

Yeah, we started looking at each other with our good eye. Frank was the very first man who, when we were about to make love, brought up the topic of contraception first.

Not after.

Not in a fevered phone call at four o'clock in the morning three weeks later:

"Hey! Remember me? Remember the time we made out? Were you using anything?"

"No."

You sweat now, pig boy!

So Frank says, "Listen, Sandra, are you using anything right now?"

"No..."

(Shit!)

He says, "Listen, just give me twenty minutes, I'll be right back."

I think he's making a dash for it. I'm like, "Where are you going?"

He says, "Just chill out, I'm going to the drugstore to buy myself some condoms."

I got misty-eyed. I'm sorry. That's just the most beautiful thing I've ever heard... Man, I would have slept with this guy now even if he'd had an axe lodged in his head!

So, he had his apartment, and I had mine. I'd sleep at his place, he'd sleep at mine; we turned into like windshield wipers, you know, back and forth. Independent, but with the same thought in mind.

We met for breakfast, and we were having coffee, and he said, "Well, you're never gonna guess, but I got my notice. They sold the house that I'm living in and I gotta be outta my apartment April 1st."

"Are you kidding? 'Cause I just got my notice, I swear to God, it was slipped under my door. When I left you last night I got home and there it was. She sold both sides of the house that I'm living in and I've got to be out by April 1st."

Frank says, "I guess I'm gonna have to find a one bedroom apartment, because my roommate is gonna go live back home, he can't afford rent in Toronto, I guess I have to find my own place. Man, a one bedroom apartment is like six or seven hundred, first and last... I'm looking at fifteen hundred. Plus telephone, fuck... It's gonna be so expensive."

"Oh, I know," I say. "'Cause I have to find a one bedroom apartment also, you know. As well. Too. And you know, Frank, when he moves out you're going to have to buy so much stuff, I mean, he's gonna take a lot of stuff with him... he's gonna almost leave you with, like, no stuff at all, and when you live alone you gotta have a lot of stuff. And I'm just saying that 'cause I have got so *much* stuff. I've got like almost two of everything. You know... okay, say... I'm just saying, say, say, let's just say we look for an apartment to share, like a two bedroom, I'm just saying... then, you know, you could use all my stuff. For free. Initially."

So, on this very heavy "stuff" platform, we discussed living together. Now, we had both lived with people prior and we found it almost necessary to stab these people in their sleep. So we went out looking for a two bedroom apartment in Toronto.

First place we go, the door swings open and the landlord is a living garbage can. He's filthy, phenomenally filthy. He stinks to high heaven so bad we're choking on it. And he can hardly speak for the bubbling ooze in the back of his throat. He finally hawks out, "Are ya here to look at the apartment?"

"Yes, Phlegm Master, we're here!"

He takes us down, down, down into the bowels of the earth.

It's a basement suite.

"How much for this little subterranean love nest?"

"Nine hundred dollars."

And it had one window right at the top of the ceiling about six inches deep and eighteen inches wide. I part the curtain.

"Oh, hey, Frank, it's got a nice view of the... garden hose."

And the more we looked and the closer we got to the crust of the earth, the more exponentially, geometrically expensive it got. And the time that we had to move out of our apartments was coming up really really quickly.

Now we get to a part where I don't remember everything that happened, so I'll tell you exactly what I remember.

I remember we woke up, and we got dressed, and we went for breakfast, and then... we bought a house.

No, we did it right! We viewed it at night, and we bought it on the strength that it had a walk-in closet.

Frank and I, in very strict discussions about the apartment, had decided exactly how much money we were going to spend. We weren't going to spend more than five or six hundred dollars. We had a real ceiling, a real budget. Boy, we had a budget! But in one hour, we spent one-hundred-and-seventy-four *thousand* dollars!

Now, if you ever want to laugh hard, really fuckin' chucklehead hard, go to a bank and try to get financing when you're a comedian and a puppeteer.

So that night, Frank and I are lying in bed

trying to come to grips with this: what the fuck did we do? Frank is lying in bed, his body twitching in shock, his eyes staring at the ceiling. I'm folded at the edge of the bed, rocking.

"Frank? Do you remember if there was a sink in the kitchen?"

I remember the day we took possession of the house. We have the key, we go to the door, we put the key in the door, we open the door. It smells like somebody else. We go in the house, we go in the kitchen, and we're standing on the linoleum in the kitchen. The linoleum in the kitchen looked like somebody had puked and then they'd spread it out really thin, and then they shellacked it.

Frank finally says, "Well, I'm gonna go down in the basement."

Fuckin' A, bubba!

"I'm gonna stay right here."

Frank comes up the stairs so quickly; his face is ashen. He's beckoning me. "Come with me."

Oh, fuck, it's a dead body. I'm sure it's a dead body.

We get down into the basement. There's five inches of water everywhere, and a hole. And the hole is just gushing up water of its own volition.

"Frank? Frank, uh, what happens here? What's happening? Frank, what's wrong with it?"

"I don't know. I'm a puppeteer!"

Fair enough!

We needed drainage experts. And in they came. The Handymen from Hell. Every single last one of them who came through that door had their pants slung down to the middle of their butts. Why, with the money you're demanding from me hourly, can't you purchase a pair of proper-fitting trousers? Must you show me the big crack in your ass? Indeed, if you must, can't you at least put it to good use? Put a pen down there or something!

Frank and I were living together

for the very first time. It's very hard to live with somebody, very hard. We were living together for the very first time, and we had a debt load that would choke a Clydesdale. And there were things happening in the house that had to be done. I'm not talking about renovation or anything cosmetic, I'm talking about upgrading a thirty-amp service so we could plug in more than a toaster.

So they'd open up a wall to do one thing, and then three more things would reveal themselves, and they *had* to be done. They had to be done. And there were holes everywhere, and the money— the money was just leaping out of every pore in our bodies and into these holes.

So, in an effort to cope with the stress I turned into... my Mother!

And Frank turned into his Dad.

And we argued every day, over every little fuckin' thing— well, because his Dad had never met my Mom!

And one day I'd just about had enough.

I think he was slicing an egg wrong.

"That's it, you fucker!"

I went into that kitchen and I commenced strafing the skin off of him, up one side, down the other. Oh, but he was ready for me. He just turned around and went "Arrrrgggghhhhhh!"

Steel cage match. Nobody gets out alive. After the fight, there was just blood and bones and snot and skin and shit and corruption hanging from every rafter in that kitchen. And all that was left of us was two sets of clanging teeth on that puke-coloured linoleum.

Frank said, "I'm outta here. I'm going for a walk."

I think he went to Whitby. Yes, and I was left all by myself in the billion-dollar house. So I decided to have a little chat with myself.

"Sandra, Sandra dear, hello? Anybody home? Sandra, darling, didn't your parents leave you a beautiful lasting legacy? Don't you know you're just not genetically predisposed to be happy, don't you know that? Must a big, big tree fall on your teeny, teeny head?"

Man, it didn't look good. So I started doing what I have always done every time I have prepared to leave. Scanning the room, I went,

"Let's see, um... that's mine... that's mine... mine... I bought that for Frank... well, fuck it, I'm taking it..."

So I turned on the TV, for light. I find that blue favours me. And there on TV, honest to God, was the National Compatibility Quiz. So, I took it, and I answered for Frank, too. There were fifty questions and how you answered them gave you an idea of what kind of relationship you had. Fifty questions, but the best one, certainly the litmus test for any relationship that I have ever had was this one:

Your partner gains fifty pounds. What do you do?

1. Nag.

2. Have an affair.

3. Express your concern and show your support. That's the one I picked.

So I'm sitting there in front of the TV. I hear the door open and close. Frank's home. He comes in the room and says, "What are you watching?"

"The National Compatibility Quiz. Here's a good question for you, Frank. Your partner gains fifty pounds. What do you do?"

And he thought about it just for a second, and he said, "Gain fifty-one."

Good answer!

Well, we looked at each other, and we started to laugh and laugh and laugh for probably the very first time since we bought the house. So, when we laugh it's a good thing, it means we're out of our slump. Oh, but there's still a steep uphill grade on that.

Now, I just got it into my big head— and I don't actually have to justify it because I'm a woman— I got it into my big head that we should get married.

So one morning at breakfast, I said, "Frank... honey... we've been getting along really good, eh? Since Tuesday it's been good, eh, Frank? You know, um, maybe we should get married... to each other."

He said, "Um, I'm not ready to get married... maybe in a couple of years... I don't know, maybe in two or three years... like maybe, five... you know I'll bet you in about five years I'll be ready to think about getting married."

I said, "Oh, good! 'Cause you'll probably be horny by then, too."

Well, I didn't like that answer very much. And I'm very creative, so I just started slipping it surreptitiously into everyday conversation:

"Well, you know, Frank, if we go see that movie at the Sheridan, it's kitty-corner to City Hall. We could get married. It just makes sense."

Finally, Frank said, "Look, right now, give me one good reason why we should get married."

Well, historically, I have no good reason to get married. So I said something pathetic, like, "Well, everybody else is!"

Wrong answer.

Frank has asthma.

He's a professional asthmatic. He has asthma, and people who have asthma sometimes get tight in the chest and they have trouble breathing, and to that end they carry a little inhaler, and they inhale on this little puffer, and then they can breathe again. But sometimes inhalers don't work and so they have to go to the hospital. So if you're ever in the presence of somebody who has asthma and they're having an asthma attack, take them to the hospital. Don't stand around like a Canadian, saying, "Well, is there something I can do?" Because they'll fuckin' die thanking you, 'cause they're Canadians, too.

So, Frank has an attack, and we go to the hospital, we go to Emergency. It's breath-related so we're ushered in right away. (Of course, this was years ago.) Frank has been issued one of those blue backless numbers which I find so fetchin' on men. I've got his jacket, I've got the pants, I've got the underwear, and I'm also doing my Mama Badger imitation: "Don't you come near my boy unless you're a trained medical professional!"

So Frank is standing there and I've got all of his stuff and he's doing up his last little modesty tie, waiting for the doctor to come in, and he turns around, and he cups my face in his hands, and he says,

"Sandra, will you marry me?"

And I say, "Yes! Yes, thank you for asking, yes!"

There, on bended lung, he proposed marriage to me. Now, when I told this story to my friends, they all went, "Oh, my God! Oh, Sandra, did he think he was dying?" Well, don't think it didn't cross my mind.

So the next morning at breakfast, I said, "Excuse me, Frank, uh, you did propose marriage to me last night, you know. You did..."

He said, "And *you* accepted."

Just checking!

So to celebrate we went out and bought Mood Engagement Rings. Makes sense when you think about it. And a big stack of magazines. Hey, that's fun for home-owners, okay?

So there we are, we're lying in bed— I'm on the woman's side, which is the furthest from the light switch. I have on my night table all the magazines I like very much. Frank is on the man's side, and he has on his night table all the magazines he likes very much. And in the middle is a little stack of stuff we both like. I'm reading *Better Homes and Gardens*: "Fifty Gifts to Make Before Christmas." No shit, I love that stuff. Oh, look here. "Sassy calico kittens to make from scraps and buttons!" I love that.

Frank is reading the *Popular Mechanics* issue that boasted the Stealth Bomber on the front. And as he's whipping through that he goes, "Oh, Sandra, there's that free-standing drill press I was telling you about." I mean, what can I say? Oooo! Oooo!

So I'm lying there in bed, and the moment descends upon me. I don't know how to describe it; it's like a walk into the Twilight Zone.

I think, *Here I am, I'm in my bedroom, in my bed*— and I had my favourite things around me that I really loved, I was on my side and I was really warm, I was looking at Frank and feeling really good, and I was thinking about all this stuff and I grabbed his arm, and I said out loud,

"Look! Look, Frank! You're a man and I'm a woman!"

Okay, I don't always let him in on the whole thing. But what I was trying to say was that here I was, in a house that I was sharing with somebody that I loved and that I liked, which as you know is extra bonus points, and that we had a life together, and I was warm and I was safe, and for the very first time in my life I realized what it was like to be happy at home.

Thank you very much.

Wedding Bell Hell

I'd like to start the evening off

by telling you about a conversation I had with a woman I thought was very important. This conversation was the result of a shopping trip Frank and I went on. I don't know if you guys do this, but Frank just lets his underwear pretty much go to nothing. There's this thick elastic and these fucking shreds hanging off it. I guess when he's tired of flossing his butt, he goes and buys underwear— a lot, at once— you know what I mean— 365 new pair, right away.

And so we were at Eaton's and he bought a heap of Jockeys, and I'm just looking at one of these pairs, and I see, attached to the fabric of the underwear itself, a little sticker. And the sticker says, "Inspected by Mildred." I thought to myself, *This Mildred must be a hell of a woman.* Imagine this job, inspecting men's underwear: stretching the elastic, making sure there's two leg holes, stuff like that.

My curiosity prompted me to call Jockey International. Their headquarters are in Kenosha, Wisconsin, and I spoke to the head of their public relations department— Barbara *Short*. No shit. That's her name.

I said, "Barbara... Mildred? Speak to me of Mildred."

And she says, "I know what you're asking and I have to tell you right away: there's no such person as Mildred. Mildred is the code name for the plant where the underwear are manufactured. So Mildred, the *plant,* is in Missouri, and Karen— another inspector name— the *plant*— is in Kentucky."

I said, "So what are you saying here, Barbara? Are you

saying that women don't make and inspect men's underwear? Are you saying that? Is that what you're saying to me?"

She said, "No, in fact, ninety-eight per cent of the people who work for Jockey are women, and all Jockey underwear are handmade by women."

Handmade. By hand. With their little hands. They make underwear, and these underwear are *hand* inspected by women. So women have their fucking hands all over those things before men even put them on!

I said, "Well, okay, you know, Barbara, now that I have you on the phone, as Public Relations Director for Jockey International, do you ever get complaints from men?"

And she said, "Well, no, not really... though when I hear from gentlemen, they do express certain concerns."

She said, "Yeah, men basically have two major concerns. Comfort and containment."

And then she offered, because I didn't even know to ask, "Oftentimes, when I receive a letter from a gentleman, there is an accompanying diagram." And the most frequent and biggest suggestion she gets is that many men feel that the basket area should be calibrated in different sizes, the same way women's bra-cup sizes are. You know, like A cup, B cup, C cup. Of course, we all know the truth. No man would ever buy an A cup.

I said, "You know, Barbara, we are approaching the year 2000. What do we hope to look for in the future of men's underwear?"

She said, "It's interesting you ask. We've just come out with a new line. Are you familiar with the fact that the pocket opening is always on the right-hand side, and vertically situated?"

And I said, "Yes, Barbara, I am well-versed in this area. Yes, I am."

She said, "The new Jockey underwear has the pocket centrally located, as usual, with the opening... horizontal."

Room for two hands. I guess that is how men will be observing the millennium.

Welcome to *Wedding Bell Hell*!

Will you marry me?

Will you... *marry me?*

Standard proposal, "Will you marry me?"

If you answer in the affirmative, "Yes, yes I'll marry you," things happen.

And if you say, "No, fuck off," then nothing happens... and you can't go back to dating, I've found!

Now, I stress the importance of the proposal. You should have yourself a proposal before you go down the aisle. I think you ought to. And I stress this because of an experience I had in Toronto at The Bay at Queen and Yonge.

Okay, I was there, at one of the cosmetic counters, and one of the women who works there was applying some kind of white-out stuff under my eyes. You know what I mean. Because I have really dark circles under my eyes, and I put that white-out stuff on, and it actually looks like I slept this year. Which is a good thing.

She's there, and she's dabbing away, and if you have ever done this or seen this, her head is always really close to you, you know, and I'm so self-conscious, so I breathe out of the side of my mouth, and *down*. Because you don't want that awful dragon breath... So I'm breathing down... and she's dabbing this stuff on my eyes, using her two ring fingers. Fingers I thought were useless up until then!

And she says to me, while dabbing, "You're never going to guess what I did today."

"Oh, no... what did you do today?"

"I bought my white wedding shoes."

"Well, congratulations! When are you getting married?"

She said, "Actually, I'm not getting married, it's just that they were on sale and I thought I might need them one day."

What kind of fucking insanity is that? You don't go around amassing white stuff! And lying back on it and just springing it on some poor bastard when he walks by! You get yourself a proposal first! Then you go shopping! It's a law.

Now, if you say yes to a proposal,

you become an engaged person, and you, as an engaged person, are fair game for every married person on the planet earth who has a little piece of advice. And they're not shy, either.

In my case, they kept coming up to me, saying, "You've got to register! For Christ's sake, get down there and register! You've got to register!"

"Register what? My breed?"

"No. You go to Birks and you pick out a pattern and you register for flatware... those are forks and knives... china... those are plates. And then there's your crystal, dear... those are glasses."

Okay, this is not my style at all. I would feel very badly if a friend of mine emptied their entire bank account and displayed the totality of their creativity and bought me a fork!

"Look, I bought you a fork!"

"And that's a good fork, too... look at that. Boy, that's a good fork. Oh, I can hardly bend that fork, that's a really good fork!"

I thought, *If you need to buy me stuff like that, Petro-Canada has a lovely Olympic glass offer.* The gold ring around the rim and those action sports figures. You can never have too many. And you can do your shopping right across Canada.

Now, to become a married person and

to do all the things it takes to become a married person— it creates *stress*. Do you know this? Stress. Do you know that they've calibrated the amount of stress that's created by wedding preparations as the same amount of stress that is created by a death in the family?

It's the kind of stress that you don't really notice. It grows incrementally. It's small, but accumulative. So you don't *really* notice. You're doing all this stuff up here, in your head. You're chatting and talking, you're making choices, you're on the phone— blah blah blah blah— and it's crawling up your body.

Suddenly you find yourself confused and shaking, and saying things like: "I just don't feel like myself." And then, as it crawls up your torso, you find yourself losing weight and sleep, and getting progressively more hysterical.

Then you get the thing in your eye. You get that thing in your eye. That thing that makes your eye twitch and pulse, *and nobody else can see it!* If it gets bad enough, your eye will start closing sideways, like elevator doors.

Now, in the Wild, Wild World of Women,

there is an occasion known as the bridal shower. I guess originally it was intended that the friends of the bride would gather to help her celebrate, and offer her gifts to start her household. Right? So if you look at the why of the shower, you can understand my confusion as to why there even exists "the stag."

"Let me get this right, honey. You went out, you drank too much, you smoked cigars, and you watched stag films. Okay, well, I'll tell you what I'm gonna do. I'm gonna make supper with all the stuff I got. And you can eat your fucking shoe, how's that?"

To attend a shower in Sudbury, Ontario,

is an entirely different thing than to attend a shower in Toronto. But I'll get to that in a moment.

Now regardless of where it is held, all showers are a secret! *Shhhhh*, it's a secret! And the bride— who is now legally insane— what she could really use right now is a surprise party!

It's the groom's job to get the bride to the shower. That's the groom's job! Because all of her friends are already there, and she's so out of her mind by now that he can drag her anywhere and she'll believe anything.

"Oh, where're we going? We're going to the library? Okay, sure, honey..."

Now in Sudbury, entrance to a shower is gained by standing at the door of the appointed house with your gift and a platter in your hands that's covered with tin-foil. That's your ticket in! And it's crinkled tin-foil, which displays a re-user mentality.

"Oh, we're not going to use our good tin-foil. No, no, no. We're saving that for something else, something special. Maybe a nice funeral."

And if you lift the tin-foil, it will usually reveal a big, shiny, honkin' Jello salad mould in lime green Jello, and in the Jello itself is embedded little corn niblets and shreds of carrots or something. Oh, there's some good eating there!

And of course, everybody brings one. The whole fucking buffet is jiggling and alive. So you bring your mould in and you put it with the rest of the moulds, so they can commune, I guess. You go in and the house is nicely decorated. There are white streamers swagged everywhere, and where they all come to-gether are those "things"— I'm not sure what they're called. Maybe they don't *have* a name. When they're collapsed, they're the shape of a boot. And when you open them, they make paper bells... I love those things! "I'm nothing! Now I'm a bell!"

Now, somewhere in the living room, there's a special chair. And this chair is covered in bows and ribbons and covered with those Kleenex roses. That's the chair where the bride is going to sit. That's the bride's chair. And right there, next to the chair, is a paper plate with two ribbons attached to it. Do you know this paper plate? None of the guys know what we're talking about!

So the bride arrives and the festivities may begin!

In Sudbury, we used to play shower games. Do you know them? Shower games are games for girls! They're girl games! And you will never see them anywhere else in the world but at a shower. And there is always one woman who *really* wants to play them! And here they come, the top three games— hold your horses. Now remember, everybody's bathed; they're dressed nicely; they've made an effort— and you know the age range at a shower is like twelve to ninety!

Okay. Two teams are established. The first game is like a race game. Everybody is told to stand and form two lines, one beside the other. And each person in each team is issued a wooden clothespin— or I've seen this played with a cocktail wienie— but that's your more high-end shower.

Each person's got their wooden clothespin. And in front of each team, at the end of the room, there are two clean jars, like mayo jars with wide mouths.

Everybody is told they have to hold the clothespin between their knees. Then, someone yells "Go!" and you have to run down to the end of the room with the clothespin still between your knees. When you get to your bottle, you pose over it, you drop your clothespin in the bottle, and you run back so the next nine-hundred-year-old woman can do the very same thing. The first team that's got all their clothespins in the jar *wins*!

It's too competitive for you, isn't it? Okay, here's a little game you can play all by yourself! You're sitting and you're chatting and you're catching up and whatever, and in comes the hostess and says:

"Girls, we're gonna play another game, okay? Whoever crosses their legs first, *loses*!"

So, in my mind, I'm always really intent on winning this game. I'm not a team player, and I think I can control my own body. So I just bend at the waist and wedge my shoulders between my knees. Fuckin' hell! This one's *mine*. But then you forget... because you're a human being. And some woman comes in with a big platter of Nanaimo bars, and you think,

Oh, I'd love one of those!

You've got to cross your legs to eat.

Last game. Same two teams. Everybody is told that they have to hold their arms behind their backs. You may not use your hands or your arms in any way, shape or form. Then the hostess comes and puts a grapefruit beneath the chin of the first person in each row. And then the first person in the row has to pass it to the woman behind her so she gets it under her chin using only her tits as leverage! Apart from the fact that this is *really* attractive, I'm sure they'll make it an Olympic sport. "Pass the pamplemousse." Wouldn't you like to see that on an Olympic tumbler at Petro-Canada? Eh?

Well, now we're all tuckered out from eating Jello, aren't we.

"Wait! There's some lovely prizes for your efforts!"

Now, at every shower there's a laundry basket, and it's decorated in the same motif as the bride's chair. Oh, now, let's see what we've got as rewards for being such good sports! Oh, here's two lovely wooden spoons, with a bow.

At this point, someone will yell out, "Well, you can never have too many wooden spoons."

Fuckin' think again, here!

"Oh, now, look at this. It's a bouquet! But it's made of copper pot scrubbers! Isn't that unique?"

And everybody "Ooooohs."

Now, this last one I've always wanted but never got. It's a six-pack of bikini panties with the days of the week embroidered on them, because I always check my genitals to see what day it is! "Ho, ho, it's been Wednesday a long time!" And there's only ever six pairs! There's no Sunday panties! No. That's the Lord's day!

Well, at a certain point they bring that addle-minded bride over, and they put her in her chair. And then a friend who can write sits next to her.

It's at this point they take that paper plate and they put it on the bride's head and they lash it to her head under her chin. Each gift is then opened, and the giver and the gift are recorded by the friend, and then the friend rips the bows and ribbons off the gift and sticks them onto the paper plate on the bride's head! This happens with every gift that is recorded and passed: the bows and the ribbons are ripped off and jammed onto the paper plate, until *all* the bows and *all* the ribbons from *all* the gifts are heaped onto the paper plate. It's her memento! And if that doesn't push that poor fuck over the edge, nothing will!

Okay, my shower was different.

It was. I had my shower in Toronto.

Now friends of mine approached me, and said, "Do you want to have a shower?"

And I said, "No, come on, guys, we've got so much stuff..."— having built my entire relationship on the "stuff" platform— "Can't we just go out for dinner?"

And they went, "No, no, well, you know, we're your friends and we'd like to offer you a shower."

I said, "Okay, well, if that's true, then, let's make it a theme shower. Let's make it a theme shower, where everybody who attends has to wear an old bridesmaid's dress."

Because I know you've got that fine garment at home. And you're mad you never got to wear it again. Could you imagine it? Every woman walking through the door has a big puffy dress on, the tits are really pointy, and she can hardly move, 'cause it's too tight... God, that would be a sorry sight. But I'd laugh.

Now, it's a really hot summer Sunday in Toronto, and Frank and I have spent most of the morning in bed. Well, we can do that because we have air conditioning.

Yeah, you know in the winter-time when it's really, really cold? Like really cold? And you get into bed and the sheets are like ice? You're so cold, you're just trying to warm up that little area around your body. As your teeth are chattering, you look at your partner and you go, "It's real cold. You know, if it was warmer, we'd make love or something, probably, right? Oh, I can't wait for this summer, when it's hot and frothy and we can make love."

Come summer-time, and you don't have air conditioning, you're lying spread-eagled in bed, and you're thinking,

Oh, you're not going to put your big leg on me, are you?

So we spent the morning in bed and the AC was on full-bore. After you make love, you get that great deep voice; you get like Barry White's voice. 'Cause your diaphragm gets such a great work-out, eh? (The diaphragm in your body. The one you were born with.)

So Frank turns to me and says in a deep tone, "You know what would be a great idea?"

I go, equally deep, "No, what would be a great idea?"

He says, "You know it would be a good idea if we rented a video."

I say, "What a great idea. And you know what else? Popcorn. Popcorn's a great idea."

116

So we're talking video, we're talking popcorn, we're am-
blin' out of bed, we're talking about, you know, what we've
seen, what's rentable right now, you know those conversations.
And we're kinda, we're just kinda, you know, easing out of
bed. And my hair is all over the place.

I've got FFL.

That Fresh-Fucked Look.

So I say to Frank, "You know, sweetheart, why don't you
go get the video, and I'll stay home and make the popcorn? By
the time you're back with the video, popcorn's ready, you
know— Bang!— it's a perfect day for a matinee."

And he says, "No, no, come with me."

"You know, honey, I would... it's just that right now, I
don't feel... *fresh!*"

And he says, "You never walk with me any more."

The most emotionally loaded sentence in any relationship.

"You never *blank* with me any more."

Whatever goes in the blank, *you've got to do it!* Right then
and there! Because if you don't, you'll suffer emotional ramifi-
cations for ten years to come!

For example:

"You never touch my dick any more!"

You've got to get on that thing like ticks on a dog; you've
got to be all over it like white on rice— until he cries uncle.

You must do it!

I see how incredibly important it is to him, so I look down
on the floor where I keep most of my clothes, and I put anything
on— "Yeah, yeah, these pants are okay,"— and I'm trying to
unwind my bra so my tits aren't colliding and I pull on my

T-shirt and I know I blew my nose in it— don't ask— and I put my hair in a pony tail.

"Okay, let's go."

Two minutes out the door, Frank says, "I forgot that cheque at Karen's."

Karen's our neighbour.

I say, "So pick it up tomorrow."

He says, "No, if I don't put it in the bank today, our mortgage cheque is going to bounce."

"Okay, we'll go pick it up, it's not a problem. We'll just slam it into the instabank next door to the video shop."

We get in front of Karen's house. Frank starts towards the door, and I stay on the sidewalk.

And he goes, "Come on, come on."

I go, "Oh, no, sweetheart... no, sweetheart, I'm just going to stay on the sidewalk, okay, honey? You know. Down wind."

And he says, "You always just stand there!"

Oh, fuckin' hell! "Okay..."

We're standing at the door.

Knock, knock, knock.

We see Karen coming towards the door.

Door opens.

"Hi, guys. What's up?"

"Well," Frank starts, "we forgot that cheque here yesterday, and if I don't put it in the bank, our mortgage cheque is going to bounce."

I say weakly, "Hi, Karen."

And she says, "Not a problem. I was going to call you."

And it's at this point he does a man thing! It's a really small thing, but we're standing at the door talking to Karen, and he puts his hand into the small of my back and he just applies a little bit of pressure. It's a really small thing, but my whole body moves forward. "What is that?" Just a little bit of pressure on the spine and the legs *go*. I don't think anything of it. I've been to Karen's a thousand times. I stumble over the threshold. We're chatting about mortgage rates, everything's fine, I don't think anything of it until we hit the living room.

And then *blammo*! All of my friends, really nicely dressed, in a huddle?

"SURPRISE!"

They all break rank and start running towards me in slow motion. Oh, no! And now I'm looking around for Frank! And I see him waving as he backs out the door...

Nooooo!

I stank to high heaven! We are talking serious, tuna-trawler time here!

Now, we'd discussed exchanging rings

during the ceremony. I thought it would be important for me to have a ring that was representative of who I was as an individual, as opposed to the institution I was about to become a part of. So to that end we went to an antique market at Harbourfront to look for rings.

So one Sunday I was down there, and I saw this ring in a really old display case, and I said to the woman, "Hi, can you show me that ring, please?"

And she takes it out, and I put it on, and I'm in awe. "Oh,

my God. It's so beautiful. Oh, it's really nice! Oh, it's nice, I like it a lot."

I call Frank. "Frank, Frank, come here. Okay, honey, look, it's good, eh? It looks good on my hand, eh? It's me, eh? Give her money!"

And he said, "You know what? It's a really nice ring. Let's just see how much it costs."

And so, attached to the ring is a teeny little tag. I have no idea how they got so many numbers on such a teeny little tag. So he flips the tag over, and right away he screams, and he gets like a fear boner at the same time!

He's yanking at my finger. "Take it off! Take it off!"

"Okay, okay, geez."

I take it off. I hand it back to the woman.

There's no way in the world that he doesn't know I love this ring. This is my ring! Mine! Mine!

Now, I don't go home and beg, "Please, oh, please, please, please? Oh, please?"

No, I don't do that. It's not my way.

No, I don't do that, but I am excellent company all week long!

The next weekend comes around, and I say, "Frank, you know, let's hop on our bikes, ride down to Harbourfront— we could use the exercise— and, you know, there might be some things— rings— we might like to see there."

And he says, "Yeah, okay, sure."

So I run right out, and I'm straddled on my bike right away, and waiting. And waiting.

And I go, "Frank, come on. Frank, come on." I ring my bell. "Frank? Come on!"

I don't know what he's doing; he's dicking around in there. He finally comes out. He gets on his bike. We go.

Saturday, summer, heavy tourists, so it's really busy. I wait until there's a break, and I step towards the same proprietor, and I say, "Hi. I don't know if you remember me? But I was here last week and I saw this really gorgeous ring... black onyx with white diamonds around it? Could you please just show me that ring again?"

And she goes, "Oh, hi! Yeah, I remember you. Sure, I remember your hair. Oh, and wasn't that a fabulous ring?"

"What?"

"Oh, I'm sorry dear, but you know, it was such a beautiful ring, I wasn't surprised when it sold. No, it's such a rare combination, you know. Oh, I'm sorry. I have to tell you that that ring is gone. It's sold."

And I started to cry. Yeah, not a little blinky cry, a big cry, a big, sobbing cry, like a child. In between gasps I kept saying,

"How could you sell my ring?

People around the counter are now backing away.

Frank's saying, "Oh, my God, what is it?"

"She sold my ring!"

He's running around me in a circle with his arms out-stretched. He's spotting me.

"Oh, my ring is gone!"

I am crying. I look on the counter and the counter is all wet. And I'm standing there crying. The woman's husband was having a coffee break, and he steps around the partition holding a bag of cookies in his hands, and he asks what the commotion is. His wife explains that I'm heartbroken over the sale of the ring, and he says, "Do you want a cookie?"

"Yes, please. I want a cookie. Yes."

I take a cookie out of the bag and place it on my ring finger. I start crying even harder.

"It's not the same!"

Now, Frank is directing me away, saying, "Come on, come on, we have to go home."

"No! No. We have to wait here."

I'm out of control! Frank's leading me around Harbour-front, trying to, like, walk me out of it, and my eyes are big red saucers in my head, and I'm crying, and he's working so hard to get my mind off it. He's trying so hard to amuse me.

And he points every once in a while to some highly desirable object and says, "Oh, look at that!"

"No! I want my ring."

I've never reacted to an object like that before in my life! I knew the ring was gone. I knew there was nothing I could do about it. I never mentioned it again.

Two weeks later, I'm at home. I'm sitting on the couch in the living room with my head resting on the coffee table.

Frank comes in and goes, "What's up?"

"I don't know. I'm just feeling low. I don't know what it is. Mostly all day I felt low. That's all it is, I just feel mostly low! I don't know, I just feel low."

And he says, "You know what? I bet you if you had a really nice long hot shower, you'd feel so much better."

"No, I don't think so. And also I have a show tonight, and I don't think they're going to pay money to see *low*!"

I laid my head on the pillow and closed my eyes.

I hear Frank leave the room. I might have heard him actually go upstairs. But I don't pay attention until I hear his voice again, and it's right in front of me.

And I hear him say, "Sandra, will you marry me?"

And I say, without even opening my eyes, "Look, I already said 'yes' once, okay, don't bug me again."

I open my eyes.

There's Frank.

He is on one bended knee. He has a little box in his hands that's cracked open, and inside is my ring! I start to scream! Right away, he got *all* the brownie points! I usually eke them out. Not this time! I just shovelled them all his way. I was so happy I got my ring.

Now here's a funny story. I know you're all going to laugh as hard as I did when I heard it. You know that Sunday afternoon, we're going down to Harbourfront again, to see the ring? Frank's in the house dicking around? What's he doing? He's calling the woman at the antique shop.

"We're coming down. She wants to see the ring. Take it out of the case and tell her *anything!*"

Yeah, I laughed my tits off when I heard that.

Now, the man's ring, Frank's ring?

That story is an entirely different one.

Oh geez, yeah!

Frank says, "Look, I want a *band* that's *plain*. I want a *plain* band."

"Okay, well, now, let me write that down so's I don't forget! Let's see now, the band you're requesting, it oughts not to be fancy. Is that what you're saying?"

We're in a jewellery shop, and I say to the shop guy, "Could you please show me this display of rings?" and he takes out some bands.

And I say to Frank, "Frank? Frank! There's some bands here. Whew! They're plain. Wow!"

So he approaches. He comes within spitting distance, with his head turned away from the ring display.

"Do you want to try one on?"

"Sure."

"Well, do you want to give me your hand?"

He extends his arm. He puts the ring on and looks at it.

Then, he starts shaking his hand, shaking really hard from the wrist.

"Yeah, I could wear *that* forever."

Then he says, "You know, I just don't wear jewellery. And, I might have to operate heavy machinery."

He's a puppeteer!

"Frank? Could we talk, could we chat? You and I? You know what? I know we decided that we would exchange rings during the ceremony, and you know what? I have my ring and if you don't want a ring, that's perfectly okay. And if you do want a ring, then you have to look for it yourself, okay? Because I can't do anything any more. I'm not functioning. Like, I'm not sleeping and I haven't had a dump in three weeks. I'm not happening. If you want a ring, honey, please look for it yourself, okay?"

And he said, "I understand. Leave it with me."

To his credit, he's a man of his word. We're at Harbourfront at a time later, and I'm looking at something, and he comes and finds me and says, "Um, listen I've seen a ring and I'd just, like... do you have a minute? I'd just like you to come and have a look at it."

And I say, "Yeah, sure, okay. Yeah, okay," totally noncommittal. Right?

So, he's leading the way; I'm walking in his path; I'm walking behind him, and I'm thinking to myself, *Whatever it is, love it! Even if it's a big gold eagle's head with a diamond in its mouth. Love it!*

We get to the counter. The young woman serving him hands him a phenomenally beautiful ring. It is a gold band with a white gold inset. Centre white diamond flanked by two blue sapphires. It's beautiful! And for a moment, God has given me a drop of maturity and I don't say it:

"Oh, *that's* plain!"

He puts the ring on and he says, "So, what do you think?"

Therapy taught me: "What do *you* think?"

"Well, I really like it."

"Well, did you give it the shake test?"

He says, "I don't think it's going to come off."

"What if you're called away at four o'clock in the morning to operate a fork lift?"

"Well, I like it."

"You know what, honey? It's really a beautiful ring and if this is the ring that you would like, it would be my honour to offer it to you as your wedding gift."

Because we'd decided that our rings would be our wedding gifts to one another. Do you know about this? I read it in the *Emily Post Book of Etiquette*, 1947 edition. I read that the bride and the groom exchange gifts. And now, in 1947 the suggested gifts from the groom to the bride were one of the following: a rope of pearls, or a roadster! And from the bride to the groom: cuff links or a nice photo of yourself in a frame. Well, okay! I'm pulling out of the drive, singing, *See the USA in your Chevrolet...*

Now, we step very gingerly,
very tentatively, into the world of the dress. On this day, and in that dress, *you will be beautiful.* There is an entire industry built on this sentence.

"On this day, and in that dress, you will be beautiful."

I guess it's because you've been a fucking troll all your life! And here's your chance, you poor ugly fuck!

When you look in wedding magazines, like *Wedding Bells, Young Bride, Modern Bride, Brides-'R'-Us,* all the women that are in those magazines with wedding dresses on are tall, confident, and serene! And you know they're not really brides. No, because real brides have panic in their eyes and shit in their pants! Oh, but that's no way to sell a dress, now, is it?

If you approach an intelligent, articulate, brilliant, beautiful, fabulous woman, just as she's about to commence wedding preparations, and you ask her,

"What are you looking for in a dress?"

she will inevitably say, "Just something plain. I'm just looking for something plain."

And that's why they make them that way. Plain. Plain, but maybe just a merengue band on the side. Watch, point a camera, do a documentary. Just point a camera at this same fabulous woman and watch as the pressure of getting married descends upon her. Watch as she turns her head incrementally towards the path of least resistance. And on her wedding day, she will appear in the aisle in the biggest, busiest, beaded son-of-a-bitch dress you ever saw, with a big fucking cowboy hat with white netting all around it, and packing pearly-handled six-shooters. "Yee-hah!"

There is a tradition amongst women that the mother of the bride will offer her wedding dress to her daughter for her wedding day. I did not have benefit of this tradition, so I went out into the world looking for my dress.

I'm in Toronto and I'm walking down the street and I pass a chi-chi-poo-poo store. Do you know this, a chi-chi-poo-poo store? It's in a chi-chi-poo-poo store where the lipless women work. Like geckos, they have independently moving eyes, and they scare the shit out of me! As I am walking by the chi-chi-poo-poo store, in the window of the chi-chi-poo-poo store, is the biggest, whitest dress in captivity! It's an easy five-and-a-half feet at the hem. And then, on either side of it, are two huge hydrofoils for ballast. And then a big Vatican or Las Vegas headdress.

I go in.

I see her there, but I don't make eye contact with her. Like that would be possible! I go in and I start looking through the wedding dresses.

Yes. I touched them!

Suddenly, she's between me and the dresses.

"Oh, is there something I can show you?"

Well, your lips would be a nice start!

She says, in a really cracked voice, "Have you made an appointment? We prefer our clientele to make an appointment."

I didn't! I didn't know! I thought it was a store!

I say weakly, "I was just walking by and I saw that wedding dress in the window, and is there anything you can tell me about it?"

"That silk creation is from Paris, France. There is a six-month waiting order. It is $4,995.00."

Five grand, five thousand dollars, for a dress you're going to wear twelve hours and leave a sweat stain in— down to your waist?!

She continues: "Might I inquire as to what your price range is?"

I said twice as much as was in my head: "Well, you know, I'll be spending in the neighbourhood of about... uh... $500.00!"

She walks away, saying, "Might I suggest you have under-budgeted?"

Hey! Did she just shit on me?

I leave the store. I'm totally dejected. I decide to walk home. Now, I'm walking down Queen Street, and right on the sidewalk on Queen Street is a sandwich sign. And it says, "Vintage Clothing— Downstairs."

So I go downstairs, and I get down there where all the dresses are squooshed together. You know, they're all packed in really tightly, and I see a sliver of white— smooshed in, all smooshed in— a short-sleeved wedding dress.

Of course, I don't touch it. Naturally. No.

The young woman who works there comes from behind the counter, and at first glance she has the biggest, most beautiful lips I've ever seen.

She's smoking a cigarette, and she says cheerfully, "Hi! Are you looking at the wedding dress? It's in excellent, excellent shape. You should try it on."

By now, I'm demented.

"Oh, but I didn't make an appointment, eh?"

She says, "You're funny!"

Yeah, I'm fucking hysterical! She takes the wedding dress and brings it into the change room, which is a refrigerator box with a big red arrow that says "Haute" on it.

And I put it on. It is an off-white, short-sleeved, scoop-necked, mid-fifties wedding dress. It's like 1955-56. It is almost down to my ankles, with a huge full skirt. It fits almost perfectly. Except for the thirty-eight-inch bust line! I thought, *I could put the TV down there!*

I come out of the refrigerator box with the wedding dress on. I've been sweating all day, I stink, I'm out of my mind, I've got this dress on, and I've got black ankle socks on with puffy legs.

She says, wide-eyed, "It looks *good* on you. You should *get* it."

So I did! My wedding dress was $15.00. Okay? The shoes I got were a pair of black suede fifties slingbacks in perfect shape, at a garage sale. Two bucks! I was ahead $4,978.00!

I had the dress altered. Seriously altered. And I had it cleaned, and I had a crinoline built for it. Stand back, I have a crinoline! A crinoline is like a super-hero slip. "That fire looks out of control. Let me at it, I have a crinoline!"

It is the day,

it is the day before my wedding. I'm upstairs in my bedroom and I see my wedding dress hanging and I think to myself,

Oh, I should just try it on. I should just put it on.

And of course, I've had lots and lots of fittings. You know? It gets in my head to do it. So I put my dress on, and of course the dress has little teeny covered buttons and loops all the way down the back. I don't know, there's six or seven thousand of them back there. So I start early. I pop the dress over my head and start to loop the buttons...

Loop... loop... loop...

I'm lifting the dress, so I can't get to some of them. So I smooth the dress down and start at the top.

Loop, loop, loop, loop...

Now I can't get to the ones in the middle. So I call up my sister, Tannia, who was my maid of armour.

I say, "Tannia, can you please come up here for a second?"

And she says, "I'm making toast."

"Get the fuck up here right now!"

Tannia comes up and she says weakly, "What?"

"Just do up these buttons for me, would you, please?"

She steps behind me, grabs a loop, grabs a button, and pulls. And I feel her pull, and pull, and pull.

"Tannia, what's going on?"

"I don't know."

"Tannia, you're a university graduate, just report what your eyes are seeing!"

"Okay, it won't go, and it's like two inches away."

Body sweat. Complete, spontaneous body sweat. I'm sure it's what happens just before you faint. But instead of fainting, I go into this weird emotional crawl space.

"Oh, no. I can't get married now. The dress doesn't fit!"

"I know! I'll get some black electrical tape and run it around and around my waist and make it look like a cummerbund."

"911! Dial 911!"

I don't eat supper. I go to bed. I wake up the next morning. I don't eat breakfast. I put the dress on, and it fits! But of course, I'm like really wobbly, right?

I come downstairs.

Frank is standing in the foyer in his tux, and he looks beautiful. And we look at each other and right away our eyes start to drown in tears.

Don't look at him!

And of course, we've been fighting every day! Isn't it lucky we're getting married?

We drive ourselves to our own ceremony.

There should be a law against that.

Frank gets in the driver's seat. I get in the back.

My dress pops up, creating a complete white-out situation.

When we get there, Frank, and my brother Michael— who is standing for Frank— go off.

And Tannia and I are sequestered in the little room.

I am terrified.

I have never been this frightened.

I've had a thousand opening nights. Never as frightening as this one day. And I didn't know that the bride got scared. I didn't know. All wedding lore points at the male, who gets nervous or gets cold feet. Hence those photographs, with the guy kneeling at the altar, with "Help" "Me" written on the soles of his shoes. I have banners of pain crossing my chest. There's a tightness wrapping itself around my neck, and I'm sure I'm about to have a heart attack. But I'm too much of a control freak to say anything.

So between clenched teeth, I say, "Do you know what, Tannia? I'm feeling a bit tense."

And Tannia says, with a blasé tone, chewing gum, "Oh, you're supposed to be tense, 'cause you're, like, the bride, right?"

Did I wake you, Tannia?

We hear the music. We go out to face the music. We are doing the bride walk. A walk you will never see in nature or in real life.

Step...feet together. Step...feet together. Step...feet together.

(Oh, yes, Mr. Johnson, I'll get those files for you immediately!)

Step...feet together. Step...feet together.

Hey, you guys, wait up for me!

Step...feet together. Step...feet together...

In my head, I hear a race-track commentator:

And they're off... and they're neck and neck, and the bridesmaid's ahead by a step!

And as soon as Tannia hits the first row of people, she turns into Ed McMahon! Meeting, greeting, shaking hands, making luncheon dates.

I'm thinking, *Tannia, get up the fucking aisle!*

I see Frank.

I see Frank.

I see Mike.

I see Frank I see Mike.

I see the minister. I see everybody. And the pressure is coming down exponentially. And the gravity of what I am doing is descending upon me! And just before it squishes me, I squirt to the side, and I think, almost cheerfully,

Oh, well. Step...feet together. *If it doesn't work out,* step...feet together... *I can always...* step...feet together... *get a divorce.*

When I got married,

I became two things I'd never been before in my whole life: a *Married... Woman.*

I should tell you immediately that I was not emotionally prepared to get married.

And I was not willing to grow up.

But let's tackle the *Married* part first, shall we? Everything I ever learned about being married I learned from my parents. You, too? Aren't we fucked up?

My parents were married through an arranged marriage. My Father was forty years old, and he was living with his Mom. And I guess she got tired of that one day, and she packed up my big Dad and took him to the old country where, out of the thousands who wrote in, my Mother's name was chosen.

My Mother was twenty. My Father was forty. They'd known each other two weeks. And then— they were married. They didn't know each other before they got married, and they never got to know each other. They didn't like each other before they got married, and they never got to like each other. And then, somehow, we were born. I can't think about that too much.

When you're a little kid,

you never question your world. You never, ever question your world. You never make qualitative or quantitative judgements about what's going on in your home or in your world. Because if it's happening in your world, in your home, it's perfectly normal.

So if your Mom says to you, "Don't bother me now, go play with the goat's head on the pentacle in the living room"— You go!

You might complain, "I hate that goat's head. It hardly has eyes any more," but you go.

We thought our lives were perfectly normal. We thought it was perfectly normal that our parents slept in two different rooms. My Mom and my Dad each had their own bedroom and it had always been that way. It's not like one day they up and separated. It had always been that way. It was part of our family's vocabulary. Mom's room, Dad's room. I mean, I didn't even get a hint into the fact that married people slept together until I was like eight years old. I was at my Auntie Ann's house one summer, and she was making her bed.

And I said, "Well, if this is your bed, where does Uncle Al sleep?"

And she said, "Well, right beside me, sweetheart."

"Oouuu! Gross!"

You know, we never questioned the fact that every time we got into the car, a huge fight would break out. And as long as the vehicle was in motion, there was screaming in the car. And when they got tired of yelling at each other, they'd take a swipe at one of us in the back seat. We never questioned the fact that our parents never exchanged a kind word or a soft smile, that any dialogue in our house was never at conversation level. We never questioned the fact that these people seemed to hate one another. We thought that's how married people lived.

Everybody has their childhood memories. They're the

places that you go sometimes if you're having a hard time as an adult. You think, *Oh, it was so much easier when we were children. Life was so much easier as a child.* And if you follow that reasoning a little bit longer, you'll actually convince yourself that it was a better place to be, and want to stay there. But you can't. And there's a reason why. Here is one of my childhood memories.

It is the long hot summer of 1967,

Centennial year, Canada's birthday. My brother Michael and I have a standing date to dig a hole in the driveway. It's just something we do. And children can have that kind of agenda, you know.

"Look, I gotta go. I gotta dig a hole, okay? Leave me alone."

I'm ten, Michael is four. And we're just out in the driveway, cruising the perfect spot to dig that will infuriate an adult the most. On account of that is how we get attention.

My Dad's in the driveway, too. He is standing in front of his brand new 1967 Dodge Monaco. And, you know, it's hot off the assembly line, but my Dad thinks it needs a little fixin'. Which is basically his anthem. It all needs a little fixin'. So, he's got the hood up and he's standing in front of the engine and he has on his summer outfit, which is all of his winter clothes, but without the top part.

My Mom is outside, too. She's watering the house. Later, she will water the sidewalk. I guess she's hoping that the sidewalk will grow, and the house will sprout an addition. I don't know. Seems idyllic, so far, doesn't it? We expect Norman Rockwell any moment now.

Well, the hood goes down on the Monaco and my Dad starts dusting his hands off as he heads towards the house. Over the din of traffic and the spray of the hose, you can hear my Mother scream, "Don't go in the house with your shoes on!"

He doesn't even look. He doesn't stop, he doesn't hesitate, he keeps walking towards the house and you can see the "Fuck you!" leap right off his shoulder.

That's all she needs! The hose goes down and it's doing that weird snaky action on the ground. She heads into the house after him. They're both in the house and the house is filled with screaming, screaming, screaming. The house isn't big enough! Bring it on outside! My Dad comes whipping out of the house. My Mom's almost right behind him, but she's not quick enough. She sees his intent, but she's not quick enough. He gets into the Monaco and locks all the doors. Now, just out of sheer tenacity and momentum, my Mother slams her body against the windshield like some demented bug. And she's screaming solid sound into the safety glass.

My Dad knows he's safe as long as the air lasts. So, just to push her, he never breaks eye contact as he leans under the driver's side seat and pulls out— a *Playboy* magazine. And my Mother goes fucking ballistic! Now she's pounding, pounding, pounding on the car, screaming, pounding, pounding. My Dad's inside the Monaco, unfurling the centrefold. To read the articles.

We watched a lot of TV.

Michael and I watched tremendous amounts of television. This window on the television was the window *out*. It was the way out of where we lived. Television programming was *consistent*: you knew what to expect. You could turn it on, you could turn it off.

Our lives, however, were unpredictable at the best of times. And I only got an inkling as to how much television I watched when a survey came around in grade four. They actually wanted to know how much television children were watching. And I remember the first calibration was one to three hours a week. Hah! I put in over twenty hours a week. I mean we clocked in as many hours as we possibly could— all day Saturday, all day Sunday. I didn't care what it was. Anything to escape where we lived.

Whenever Michael and I watched TV, things that would make us laugh were the best, because laughter was in short supply where we lived. So, if something made us laugh, it immediately became something to worship. Saturday mornings at our house were holy.

We'd wake up really early, like seven a.m. We'd still have our pyjamas on. We'd sit in front of the TV eating a whole box of Captain Crunch, alternating between milk and the addition of more cereal. And we'd never get up to pee, in case we missed something. We watched old Abbott and Costello movies and Ma and Pa Kettle movies. And Francis the Talking Mule and old movies like that. We watched and watched and waited, because we knew Bugs Bunny was coming. Bugs Bunny was the best. We used to memorize huge pieces of Bugs Bunny.

We tried to do the voices. We tried to do all the sounds with our mouths, to imitate Bugs Bunny, because in our house, when it was really bad, we would speak Bugs Bunny to each other and try to make each other laugh. So if my Mother had been particularly hard on Michael, I'd find him and I'd say, "What's in the basket, Prissy, a husband?"

And Michael would say, "Yes!"

We still do it. As recently as when I got married. I was lying on the couch at home, and my head was on an angle so that as I was crying, tears were pooling in my ears. I hate that.

So I hear the phone ring, and I pick it up, and the voice sounds like it's coming from under water: "Hello? It's Mike!"

He says, "Listen, we're about to leave, we're here in Sudbury and we're about to come down for your wedding. Is there anything you need?"

"Mike, Michael, can you please do the Hatfield and McCoy square dance from Bugs Bunny for me, please?"

And he says, "Yeah, sure! Trout, trout, pretty little trout, splash around and come right out, de de duh de de de..."

I smile, I smile. Ah, relief!

My parents finally divorced.

Thank God! I think the worst part of living in an environment like that is the silence of it. We were told point-blank, "Never ever ever talk about what goes on in this house to anybody, ever!"

So we became the keepers of the secret. And of course, having never spoken of it, even to each other, until recently, it isolated us from one another and it isolated us from the rest of the world. Honest to God, I thought everybody else but me had a really healthy, wholesome emotional life. I thought we were the only ones who lived in a really twisted place.

When I got married, I think I really wanted to believe that I would live happily ever after. And that's not what happened. No, what happened was that my past came hurtling forward to predict my future. As a result of my upbringing and my lovely parents, I am a carrier of the divorce gene. I know how to make a divorce. I do. I know all the diminishment, I know all the manipulation, I know the scheming. Why wouldn't I? I watched two professionals work at it every day for fifteen years!

I can pick a fight.

"What do you think you're doing? You're not going to cut that onion that way, are you?"

So simple.

But that's all I know how to do, apparently. When I got married, at one end of an emotional spectrum, I couldn't believe that I loved somebody so much, and that they loved me back. See, the happy side-effect of the divorce gene is that you can't trust your own feelings and trust and believe that other people have good feelings for you. So, of course, I couldn't believe that I loved somebody so much.

And anybody I love, of course, is gonna die. And I kept thinking Frank was gonna die.

Every time he'd pull out of the driveway, I'd start crying, and think: *Oh, look, he's dead again!*

He'd drive the car out of sight, and right away it would

start. The horrible little movie in my head. Cops pull up, they knock on my door, I open the door, they tell me Frank is dead, I fall apart, a friend of mine comes, puts me back together, puts me in a black dress, and then we're at the funeral. At the funeral, I'm surrounded by my wonderful friends, and I am keening. And it doesn't stop there, no. It starts all over again. The cops pull up...

But by now I've decided what to wear.

I was terrorizing myself. I was terrified and I didn't know what to do, and I thought, *Maybe if I say it out loud, it'll stop.*

So I said, "Frank, sometimes I think you're gonna die."

And he said, "Try to keep a good thought, eh?"

And I said, "Don't you ever think I'm gonna die?"

He said, "Sometimes, sometimes."

"Frank, are you ever at the funeral?"

He said, "No, actually, I'm dating... I can't think about you dying. So you've died, I've gone to your funeral, I've met some of your fabulous friends there, and now I'm dating some of them."

Well, at least he paints himself a rosier future than me, stuck at his funeral for the entirety of my life.

So that's one end of the spectrum. The other end is a very small place. There's not much room for anything in this place. It's like a place where there's no more *nice*, like there's no more *please* and *thank you*. It's a mean, awful place. In this place, a sentence like,

"Frank, could you please pass me the sugar?"

turns into,

"Pass me the sugar! C'mon! Can't you see I need sugar? What the fuck's wrong with you? Got a fuckin' piano tied to your fuckin' ass?"

So I just oscillated between these two points. Yes, I was easy to live with. And I watched me replicate the only behaviour I knew. I watched me make all the preparations for a divorce. It's not what I wanted to do; it seemed to be the only thing I knew how to do.

"So, Sandra, what are you doing here? Are you trying to make yourself a divorce?"

"Make a divorce? Are you going to divorce Frank? Are you going to leave this great guy? And then what are you going to do? Take your long, ugly bag of shit and go offer it to somebody else?"

I had to change.

Have you ever tried to change?

I mean, even just your mind? It's really, really hard. And I knew I wouldn't do it by myself; I knew I needed help. So I called five therapists, and I left a message on each one of their machines: "My name is Sandra. I need mental help."

I had an appointment with one therapist and I went to his nice office. And I sat down in his very nice chair.

And I sat with him and I said, "Look, even before you launch into this, I'm gonna tell you how this is all gonna go. If this process of therapy gets me all emotionally on the right track and everything, but I lose my sense of humour, I want no part of it. Okay? I'd rather be fucked up and funny!"

He said, "So, what I hear you saying is that you feel your sense of humour is entirely predicated on the fact that you had a dysfunctional childhood."

"Yeah. So? You say it like it's a bad thing!"

When I first went into therapy, I thought, *Three weeks, we'll get this down in three weeks.* After three weeks, I signed up for the lifelong subscription.

All right, now, the *Woman* part.

This is not so easy. You can't just be taller, and have boobs, but have an eleven-year-old at your emotional wheel— "Are we there yet?"— steering you out of control, barely able to see over the dash of life.

You can't do that. You can't go to Women'R'Us and become an adult. When I was younger, or maybe I should just say shorter, I was taught to do everything that the women in my world knew how to do. I was taught how to cook, I was taught how to sew, I was taught how to knit. Hang on. I... can crochet... a doily. Now, I like to do those things, and I like knowing how to do those things, except that the only reason I was taught those things was that those were the only ways I was ever going to express my creativity. Oh, geez, yeah! Well, I was never going to get a job, no, no, I was never going to leave the house. No. I had a future of staying in the house, sitting in front of the TV, crocheting something nice and crying while watching figure skating.

I left home when I was about sixteen years old,
and I met my best friend, Sherry. Sherry and I were ilk, and we made each other laugh a lot, and it was that really sweet, teenaged laughter that makes adult women crazy when they hear it. Do you know this sound? And eventually, adult women are prompted to say, "What the hell are you laughing at? There's just nothing funny here!" Well, not for you, you old bag!

One time, Sherry and I are driving her dad's truck. Sherry's driving, I'm on the passenger side, the windows are rolled down, it's a Sudbury summer day, and I've got my arm out the window, my Export "A"s tucked right into the shoulder of my T-shirt. Sherry's doing the very same thing on her side, and we've got the French channel on really loud... I don't know, we just thought that was funny.

And we're driving.

Sherry says, "Look at this guy ahead of me— he's driving like a fucking maniac. I can barely keep up with him!"

Screaming, laughing, driving...

We hear a police siren...

And we get pulled over by a cop.

As we're pulling over, Sherry says, "Don't laugh, don't laugh, don't laugh."

And of course, I want to, really hard. Even now, in the face of authority, I want to laugh really hard.

So he pulls up behind us, and we see Johnny Law step out of his car. And he starts aiming towards our truck; he has on his uniform and those mirrored sunglasses, and now his face is framed in the driver's side window, and he says to Sherry, "Do you have any idea how fast you were going?"

C.Johnson Bookseller
623 Richmond Street
London, Ontario
N6A 3G5
1-519-432-4283
1-800-661-4691
GST - 10118 5510 RT

Sat Jan31-98 5:01pm
Inv#109751 CL:T

Title/ISBN	Qty	Price	Disc	Total	Tax
TRILOGY OF PERFORMANCES					
1551280442	1	17.95		17.95	1

	Subtotal	17.95
	GST (Tx1)	1.26
Items	1 Total	19.21
	Cash	20.26
	Change Due	1.05

Serious.

And Sherry says, "Gee, Officer, I guess I didn't get a chance to look at the speedometer."

He tells her how fast she was going, and he says, "You were clearly speeding in this area. I'm gonna have to give you a ticket."

And Sherry says, "Oh, don't bother, I never win on those things."

And now I'm sure we're both bleeding from the eyes with laughter. We look at him, and that stoic, stoic face of authority cracks the tiniest smile, and he says, as he waves us on, "Don't let it happen again."

Now, Sherry and I had a lot of trouble

understanding girls. Girls. "Curly Girls," we called them, the ones that giggled. And they were lithe and pliable and jiggled. Like they had too much cartilage or something, I don't know what— no bones— like a fillet of girl, if you will. And they were coy and enchanting and boys were drawn to them and they had no trouble wearing pastels.

By sharp contrast, Sherry and I were hip, cool. We drank, we smoked, we did drugs, we swore, *and* we didn't get laid until we were eighteen years old, because— who would come near us?

I genuinely thought sleeping with guys would bring out my delicate side.

You see, it made perfect sense, because in our world, boys were for *sex!* Sex! And girls were for everything else. They were for talking, laughing, crying, confiding, eating, drinking, everything, shopping, everything, everything, everything, and boys were for sex! That's all they were good for, was sex.

The phone rings.

"Hello? Oh, hi, Sherry! No, you're not interrupting, we're finished, yeah. No, I swear. Look, he's wiping his dick on the curtain. We're done. Yeah, okay, I'll meet you at Tim Hortons and we'll talk about him."

Ah, sweet youth!

Are you familiar with the *Pygmalion* theme,

the reason there is a *My Fair Lady*? The *Pygmalion* theme— the *My Fair Lady* theme— for those of you who don't know, is: basically, a guy goes over to the gutter where all women always are, and he takes something out of the gutter, and he brings it into his world, and he transforms it into a woman, and then a lady. Second degree of difficulty.

Now, a lot has been done on this very scenario in a lot of ways, but I think the best scenario that I ever saw was how they handled this sensitive issue on *Bonanza*. Ben Cartwright had three sons: Adam, Hoss, and Little Joe. I was in love with Little Joe. God, I loved Little Joe. Frank admitted an admiration for Hoss, and Sherry told me, years later, she liked Candy. The hired hand. You remember Candy? He wasn't even a Cartwright! For Christ's sake, Sherry, you gotta pick a Cartwright!

The scenario unfolds as follows: Hoss and Little Joe are in town, after buying or selling some wheat or beef, or both. And they're in the saloon, celebrating their happy exchange. Out in the street, there's a big kerfuffle, and there's an older guy rasslin' around in the mud with a younger guy. The Cartwrights, who are the most curious people on the planet, come out, and they see that this is wrong, and they insinuate themselves. Hoss has got the older guy and Little Joe's got the young guy by the waist. And there's lots of screamin' and pitchin' and yankin' and they're yellin' at one another, and you understand through dialogue that the two rasslers are related. And as the boy is yankin' and pitchin', he knocks his own hat off to reveal a wealth of chestnut hair.

"Hey, dadburn it, Hoss! It's a girl! Can I keep her?"

Well, it's clearly unacceptable that this man is beating his daughter in the street, so the Cartwrights make that moral decision to take her back to the Ponderosa. Oh, she's yankin' and pitchin' and screamin'. She's a wild one, eh? They get good Mrs. Miller from down the road— which has got to be Mexico, because the Ponderosa's so huge— to come up and help them out.

Now, the next scene is that freestanding metal bathtub. Do you know it? There's suds in it, and that hellion's in it, and she's kickin' and splashin', but her hair's all piled up on her head and there's heavy tendril action comin' down. Oh, but she doesn't like this water— she's splashin' and kickin' and screamin'— but Mrs. Miller's got her in a fuckin' headlock, and she's scraping the shit off her!

Meanwhile, all the Cartwrights are pacing back and forth in front of the fireplace. I don't know why. I guess that's what men do when women bathe. Mrs. Miller emerges at the top of the stairs and she's tucking a lock of errant hair back in, showing she had a hard time.

"Well, Ben, I've done all I can. It's up to you boys, now."

And out comes that hellion, clean and coiffed and wearing a calico dress. I think it's Adam's. Well, all the Cartwrights are mighty impressed with this metamorphosis, and they're yanking on their bolos bigtime, you know what I mean? She starts down the staircase, and Little Joe right away sticks out his arm. She takes his arm and he leads her towards the dining table, where Hop Sing has made another one of his country's favourite dishes, chicken pot pie! Cantonese-style chicken pot pie.

All the Cartwrights have impeccable manners— right away with the serviettes on their laps— and they're about to grab their cutlery. She is, of course, feral, and was raised by chickens somewhere, and she's pecking at her food, she's grabbing for stuff, and her elbows are going wild. Frankly, she's scaring the Cartwrights! Little Joe takes her hand and he puts it on a fork; he puts it on a knife— and right away, she has European manners. Hot diggedy. So what happens? They fall in love. Natch.

The next scene, you see that big calico number spread out on a grassy knoll, and Little Joe's got his head on her lap, and he's languishing on the grass. He's got no hat on and he's chewing straw, which is how you can tell a Cartwright is in love.

Meanwhile, back at the Ponderosa, her Pa's been sprung; he's come back for her, and he's dog dirty and loaded for bear.

"Ben, you gots to give me back my daughter! She's my only kin. I ain't et nor slept nor wiped myself in three weeks!"

Okay, the guy is a serious waste of skin.

Little Joe and the hellion come back from the grassy knoll in the buggy with the fringe on top, and she recognizes her Pa's horse in front of the house. Right away she's a-scared, and she tucks in behind Little Joe. Her Pa comes out of the Ponderosa and there's a big to-do, yellin' and yellin' and yellin' and they're yellin' back and forth, and right away he pulls a gun on Little Joe!

And what does she do?

She steps in front and she takes a bullet for Little Joe! Bring up *Bonanza* theme music! Dun da da dun da da dun da da dun... *Bonanza*!

Oh, they like women on the Ponderosa. Yeah, they go through them like fuckin' peanuts! Do you know the *why* of Bonanza? Ben Cartwright had three sons by three different women, which explains why these three guys look so bizarre standing next to one another. It's the truth. And, all of these women that Ben Cartwright impregnated died in childbirth. The guy is the fuckin' grim reaper, man! Try to think of something a little more horrific than Ben coming to court!

I've always wanted to be in the presence

of a woman who, at a certain point in my life, took me aside and sat me down and told it to me straight. Just gave me some of the answers to the millions of questions that come when you're trying to grow up. Somebody like a fairy godmother person, but not somebody who made vehicles from squash. No. Somebody with a brain, you know? I used to think, *If I had a fairy godmother, what would* my *fairy godmother look like?*

My fairy godmother. My fairy godmother wears a grey serge suit and she has nude nylons, black pumps, and she has dark red hair that is piled up a little bit on her head. And she has gin on her breath. Her lipstick is a little bit outside the line. And she smokes cigarettes.

Lighting a cigarette, she says to me, "Oh, now, look at you! Look at you, you're as cute as a bug's ear, look at you! Oh, my God, what I'd give to have a head of hair like that. 'Course you realize, with that hair you get a bit of a moustache, eh? Oh, but you're not the only one, no you're not. A little later on you'll start getting that hair on your chin. Oh, that's stiff ugly stuff, that is. Oh, but you're not the only one, no you're not. You ever see a woman with her finger on her chin, moving it back and forth absentmindedly, that little movement is the salute to whiskered women. No, you're not the only one, I tell you right now. If we took every little tweezer and razor, if we took all those things away right now, we'd all look like Hobbit people.

"Now, you're gonna grow up, you know you will, you will. I know it seems impossible to believe, but you will, sweetheart. You'll grow up and become a woman. And becoming a woman is all about choice, it is— oh, you've got to make those choices. You do, you do. You've got to make those choices, my dear, and I'll tell you why. Because if you don't, there's a long line-up of people who'd love to make those choices for you. Let's take your moustache, for instance. You can let all that hair grow in and then you can tell the world to kiss your ass, or we can take you down to Little Lola's House of Wax and have that sucker ripped right off! That's your choice, my darling, you gotta make it.

"Now, I noticed the other day, I wasn't gonna say it, I noticed the other day you were having a little trouble deciding where to stop shaving on your legs. Now again, you're *not* the only one. No, you're not. But in your case, poor baby, when you stopped right there at your knees, you looked like you had cycling shorts on. Rule of thumb, wherever the hem, shave six inches above. In the winter, an opaque stocking is your saviour.

"Now, you love to buy shoes, don't you? Oh, gee, you do, you do. You love to buy shoes, and you'll buy a shoe that looks lovely on your foot. A nice high heel makes your leg look longer. You love to have that shoe on your foot, but your dogs are gonna bark! Oh, and you'll be in a social situation and your feet will be *screaming*. But will you take your shoe off? No, no, no, you won't, no no no you won't, because your feet are bleeding, that's why.

"Now, you might decide to have sex. That's a choice. And you might decide to have sex with a man. That's another choice. If you opt for the man you must use contraception. You must. You don't have a special papal dispensation. No, you don't. Now you must use a condom 'cause there's AIDS, or you'll have lunch with Elvis quicker than you'd like.

"Now, remember three things: Don't look for yourself in a magazine. *You* are not there. Two: no one *ever* said, 'What a slimming plaid,' And finally: never ever ever let a friend do a perm."

So how do you know you're growing up?

In my case, there were really teeny little ways that were so important to me. I remember the very first one— it wouldn't have meant anything to anybody else but me. I was invited out for dinner at a friend's house, and I went to their house and sat in the living room next to the candy dish. And I didn't eat them all.

I remember other stuff, like the first Monday I didn't start a diet. That was really important. I can't remember them all but they were little teeny ones and they were sort of cumulative, you know? But I absolutely knew that I was becoming a woman the very first time I did this: I blew my nose with a Kleenex, and stuffed it into my sleeve at my wrist. Okay, it's not just that I did it, but I thought it was a great idea!

Time to go. This story has no end.

So before I go, I'd like to offer you a piece of advice from a married woman.

"Will you marry me?"

Not easy words to say, not easy words to hear, a choice to say yes or no. If you ever have the opportunity to say these words to someone, or hear these words and respond *yes*, take a moment and write down why. Just take a moment to yourself and on a little piece of paper, write down why. Write down why you said what you said, write down why you said it to that person, and write down why you like that person, and why you love that person— they should be two different reasons, by the way— and write down what your hopes are and what your dreams are. Write down why you said yes, why you didn't say no. Write down the courage that you had to summon to say what you did.

Write everything down, and put it in a little envelope, and ask a trusted friend to hold it for you. Because to say, "Will you marry me?" and to respond "Yes, I will marry you," is so *big,* and it's out loud and it goes right up to the universe, and almost everything that happens after you say "Will you marry me?" and hear "Yes," has nothing to do with the proposal. And the further you get away from the proposal, the less likely you are to remember why you said it, and the less likely you are to remember why you said yes. You'll start to doubt yourself, and you'll start to wonder why you even bothered to begin with, and why everything is not right, and you'll wonder why you're experiencing the confusion and the tension that you are. And you'll get scared.

When that happens, and it *will* happen, call your friend and ask them to bring you the letter, and open the letter and read for yourself *why.* Read why you said what you said, read why you love that person and why you like that person, read the confidence that you had to summon just to respond— read it— and read why it's always a better idea to be in the presence of love.

I didn't have an opportunity to write this letter before I got married because I didn't do my emotional homework before I got married. I had to do it after. Quick.

So if I had the opportunity to write this letter, this is exactly what I would write:

I said yes to Frank's proposal because, in my mind, it was an opportunity for me to belong. It was a chance, maybe, to dare that I would be able to have a house and a home that would be a safe place for me to finally grow up and become the person I was supposed to be before that detour called my childhood happened. I married Frank because he's the funniest man I ever met in my whole life, and even if things are really bad, we still manage to laugh, and sometimes I remember something that he said, and I'll be driving by myself and I'll remember, and then I'll laugh by myself in the truck. Maybe you've seen me.

And finally, I married Frank because Frank will always, always, stop and ask for directions if we are lost.

Good night!